WESLEY : A Man with a Concern

WESLEY:

A Man with a Concern

By E. DOUGLAS BEBB
M.A., Ph.D. (Sheffield)
B.Litt. (Oxon)

WIPF & STOCK · Eugene, Oregon

Wipf and Stock Publishers
199 W 8th Ave, Suite 3
Eugene, OR 97401

Wesley
A Man with a Concern
By Bebb, E. Douglas
Copyright©1950 Methodist Publishing - Epworth Press
ISBN 13: 978-1-5326-0026-5
Publication date 6/15/2016
Previously published by Epworth Press, 1950

Every effort has been made to trace the current copyright owner of this publication but without success. If you have any information or interest in the copyright, please contact the publishers.

TO
ELEANOR POTTER
MY MOTHER-IN-LAW, OF BLESSED MEMORY,

AND

GEORGE WILLIAM POTTER
MY FATHER-IN-LAW AND FRIEND

CONTENTS

ABBREVIATIONS viii

1. THE BEGINNINGS OF WESLEY'S SOCIAL CONCERN . 1

2. WESLEY'S EVANGELICAL CONVERSION AND HIS SOCIAL CONCERN 14

3. SOCIAL IMPLICATIONS OF CERTAIN DOCTRINES WESLEY COMMONLY TAUGHT . . . 27

4. WESLEY'S GENERAL SOCIAL AND ECONOMIC CONCERN 41

5. WESLEY'S CONCERN WITH CERTAIN SOCIAL QUESTIONS 57

6. WESLEY'S CONCERN WITH CERTAIN ECONOMIC QUESTIONS 108

7. THE INFLUENCE OF A MAN DEEPLY CONCERNED . 120

Abbreviations

The following abbreviations are used:

Journal: *The Journal of the Rev. John Wesley, A.M.*
In 8 vols., edited by Nehemiah Curnock (1909).

Letters: *The Letters of John Wesley.*
In 8 vols., Standard Edition, by John Telford (1931).

Sermons: *The Standard Sermons of John Wesley.*
In 2 vols., annotated by Edward H. Sugden (1921).

Works: *The Works of the Rev. John Wesley.*
In 14 vols., 11th Edition, by Jackson (1856).

Chapter One

The Beginnings of Wesley's Social Concern

INTRODUCTION

THE IMPORTANCE of John Wesley as a social factor in the eighteenth century is now widely recognized, some historians going so far as to give him primacy of place amongst those who sensibly affected the social outlook and conduct of that century with which his own life was almost coterminous. In doing this, some regard him as essentially a conservative factor, without whom England might have gone the way of the French Revolution, or at least have shown disturbing repercussions to it. Others, on the contrary, regard him more from the point of view of a social pioneer, a leader in popular education and in the development among the masses of the sense of personal worth and responsibility, and powerfully affecting such movements as the abolition of slavery and the reform of the prison system.

Whatever estimate we may finally place upon Wesley as an effective social reformer and as an exponent of decided views on economic questions, it is important to note that there are three elements which may not be overlooked in any such evaluation. They are: his ancestry and upbringing; his personal character and early experiences; his religious practice and teaching.

ANCESTRY AND UPBRINGING

On his father's side, Wesley's great-grandfather, Bartholomew Wesley, was one of the ejected clergymen of 1662; his grandfather, John, who predeceased Bartholomew, also suffered under the Act of Uniformity. On his mother's side, his grandfather was Dr. Annesley, and his grandmother's father was Mr. White, 'sometime Chairman of the Assembly of Divines'.[1] The Annesleys were related to the Anglesey family.[2]

The most marked feature of Wesley's upbringing was its almost continuous state of poverty. His father fought poverty and debt, for the most part unsuccessfully, all through his life. In a letter which he wrote to Dr. Goodall, dated the 22nd August 1692, Samuel Wesley tells how, when an undergraduate at Oxford, he was reduced to 2*d*., and this he gave to a hungry child. The same day, however, some one 'brought me a crown for a Token from one of My Relations with which I bought bread, and ye same day I think, or ye next, my Mother sent me a Cheese from London. Now I was stored against a Siege, since liquor I could not want, having ye whole Pump at my dispos wch (*sic*) was just against my Door. . . . Thus I liv'd from about Christmas to ye 14th of Febr'.[3] He had married Susanna Annesley on 12th November 1688, when a curate in London on £30 per annum. She brought no dowry and on her father's death received under his will precisely one shilling. Samuel Wesley obtained the living of South Ormsby in 1691, which was worth £50 per annum, and in 1697 some influence procured for him the

[1] Quoted from a letter written by John Wesley to Charles Wesley, in 1768. See, *Letters*, V.76.

[2] It is interesting to note that Daniel Defoe may have married another of Dr. Annesley's daughters and would be, in that case, Wesley's uncle, but there is considerable doubt about the early history of Defoe's wife (see *Dict. Nat. Biog.*, article 'Defoe'). Defoe was not only the author of *Robinson Crusoe*, but a Dissenter who was a writer on many social and economic problems and a most versatile political pamphleteer and wire-puller. Wesley does not appear, however, to have had much, if anything, to do with Defoe.

[3] Quoted from Augustin Légèr: *La Jeunesse de Wesley*, 'Pièces Justificatives', pp. 8–9.

rectorship of the parish of Epworth, a living in the gift of the Crown, worth £200 per annum, less £30 charges, and having some glebe land as well. The Epworth living, having regard to the much greater value of money in that period than now, looked comfortable, but Samuel Wesley had got into debt while at South Ormsby, and had to borrow more money to pay for furniture for the Rectory. Minor disasters, and some more important, were frequently suffered by the Rector. Burnt flax on the glebe, maimed cattle in his barns, the burning of the Rectory and loss of all their possessions, due, the Rector believed, largely to the hostility which he had aroused in the Fen folk by his uncompromising sternness with them. Above all, Samuel Wesley was a poor manager and improvident, and debts accumulated, as also did his family. There were nineteen children born between the years 1690 and 1710, of whom only nine grew to adulthood. His eldest daughter Emily, who was often the housekeeper at the Rectory, gives a bitter first-hand impression of its poverty, and of its real cause—her father. ' After the fire, when I was seventeen years old,' she says, ' I was left alone with my mother and lived easy for one year—but after we were gotten into our house and all the family settled, in about a year's time, I began to find out that we were ruined. Then came on London journeys, Convocations of blessed memory, that for seven winters my father was at London and we at home in intolerable want and affliction; then I learnt what it was to seek money for bread, seldom having any without such hardships in getting it that much abated the pleasure of it. Thus we went on growing worse and worse; all of us children in scandalous want of necessaries for years together; vast income but no comfort or credit with it.'[4] That Emily Wesley should

[4] Quoted: G. Elsie Harrison, *Son to Susanna*, pp. 39-40.

regard £170 per annum plus the small profits of the glebe as 'vast income' is itself significant, even when allowance is made for the difference in the value of money in the eighteenth and the twentieth centuries.

The Rector was imprisoned in Lincoln Castle for a debt of £30 owing to a man named Pinder and there he remained for three months until by the intervention of the Archbishop of York, Dr. Sharp, a subscription was made whereby £184 was raised toward paying off his debts which amounted to a total of about £300. When he died in 1735, he had nothing to leave his widow except £100 of debt, and some scholarly works of little or no pecuniary value. She herself only escaped imprisonment for debt in 1736 through the efforts of her son Samuel and two friends who between them provided between £65 and £70.[5]

Besides poverty, there was another marked feature of the years of John Wesley's upbringing and that was the remarkable character of his mother Susanna, and the training which she gave to her children at home. She herself had been brought up sternly to possess a great sense of duty. When she was married, her father, Dr. Annesley, remarked, ' the comforts of marriage have their whole dependence upon the performance of the duties '.[6] Such comforts as she was to know were certainly of that sort, nor did she ever allow herself to be deflected from the minute ordering of her life and the lives of her children, not even by the equally constant child-bearing and grinding poverty. Her influence upon John is abundantly testified by his own strict regimentation of life and by the way in which he used to consult his mother as to the course of action he should take when he

[5] *Letters*, I.203.
[6] Quoted: Marjorie Bowen, *Wrestling Jacob*, p. 10.

THE BEGINNINGS OF WESLEY'S SOCIAL CONCERN 5

was in doubt. Mrs. Wesley believed in the complete regulation of life, with rigid rules for all occasions, especially rigid in the use of time, accompanied by the inculcation of the most methodical habits, even from the age of four years. Her constant problem of managing for so many on so little was matched by another problem no less pressing, that of so managing them that they might all be saved. In the Epworth Rectory the future was always a source of anxiety, in respect of material necessities regarding this life, and in respect of the necessity of obtaining salvation regarding the life to come. And just as throughout his life, John Wesley ever maintained the utmost sensitiveness to the right use of money and time, so he was constantly concerned with the problem of salvation, his own and that of others. This might have developed into an intense egocentricity instead of becoming, as it did quite early in his career, a concern for others which embraced, not only their eternal welfare, but their temporal well-being. 'The Gospel of Christ', he wrote in his Preface to the Hymn Book of 1739, ' knows of no religion but social, no holiness but social holiness.' His experiences at Oxford, and still more his experiences in Georgia, powerfully affected this strand in his own highly developed individuality.

ACTIVITIES WHILE AT OXFORD

At the age of ten years, John Wesley went to Charterhouse, where he lived mostly on bread, and in 1720 to Christ Church, Oxford, as an Exhibitioner. He graduated in 1724, was ordained deacon by the Bishop of Oxford in 1725, and in March of the following year was elected Fellow of Lincoln.[7] Except for a little over two years, between 1727 and 1729, he was at Oxford until

[7] *Letters*, VIII.281; *Journal*, I.59.

1735. During the thirteen years he was actually at the University, Wesley's concern for his own soul, and those of others also seriously minded, found expression in the fellowship, rules, and practices of the famous 'Holy Club'. The strictness with which he, as the leading member of this coterie, kept the religious obligations of his Church and engaged in almost constant self-analysis, was prevented from becoming a mere self-absorption by the earnestness with which he discharged the duties of his Fellowship and the social work on which he soon became engaged. Like his father before him, he felt it his duty to visit regularly the prisoners in the Castle and Bocardo gaols and in addition he began to teach little pauper children. In the Castle, he and other 'Methodists', as they had already come to be known, held services at least three times a week, while also helping the prisoners with medicines and books, and in some cases, where the debt was small, paying it and securing the release of the debtor.

An eyewitness account, by a non-sympathizer, confirms this. Young Morgan, the youthful brother of William Morgan who while a member of the Holy Club had become insane and then died, wrote: 'They imagine they cannot be saved if they do not spend every hour, nay minute, of their lives in the service of God—they almost starve themselves in order to be able to relieve the poor and buy books for their conversion. They endeavour to reform notorious whores and allay spirits in haunted houses.'[8]

Oxford laid the foundations of this personal social service which continued in after years, however great might be the calls upon Wesley's time. The words of our Lord distinguishing those who visited and those who did

[8] Quoted: G. Elsie Harrison, op. cit., p. 86.

not visit prisoners,[9] he took very seriously and literally, and this visitation was particularly marked in the case of those in condemned cells, with whose souls they—Wesley and his followers—would wrestle to the last hour.

Already at Oxford there stands out in John Wesley his unceasing likeness to his mother—a likeness shown in his extremely methodical habits, his scrupulosity, his organizing ability, his skill in the management of money, his iron control of himself and others. That he was greatly indebted to her is hardly to be disputed, and her influence on Methodism through him has come to be widely recognized. His letters to her are very revealing, because they show a blend of filial concern and love, desire for advice, and a sharing of ideas and ideals. In other words, they are the letters of a man, not only on the best of terms with his mother, but also one who valued greatly and constantly her views and judgement. He betrays not the slightest sign of constraint but, on the contrary, is perfectly open with her. Even his early love affair in Georgia, curious and juvenile as it was, he recounts quite factually and frankly to his mother. Conversely, her accounts of her domestic life, with its great concern for the salvation of the souls committed to her, her sharp sense of responsibility for every hour of every day, and for every penny spent, and her meticulous attention to details and orderly effort, are so characteristic of her son as to make the view inescapable that in these things he was greatly influenced by his mother's upbringing.

Yet it is noteworthy that John Wesley followed his father to Oxford and like him became a clergyman loyal to the Hanoverians (unlike, at this point, his mother, who was Jacobite in sympathies), and went out as a missionary, as his father had wanted also to do. Like his father, too,

[9] Matthew 25^{36}, ^{39}, ^{43}, ^{44}.

he was a voluminous writer, albeit one very much more effective. It is also noteworthy that one of the last things said by his father while dying was: 'The inward witness, son! *That* is the strongest proof of Christianity!'[10] This, thirty years later, became a main plank in Wesley's teaching.[11] Most remarkable of all is the similarity between John Wesley's universal outlook on his mission —'The World is my Parish'—and his father's outlook as vouched for by a contemporary who was also a fellow worker with him on the *Athenian Gazette*, a weekly publication which lived some years in the last decade of the seventeenth century. This man, Charles Gildon, wrote of Samuel Wesley: 'Were it possible for any man to act the part of a universal priest, he would certainly deem it his duty to take care of the spiritual good of all mankind.'[12] Having regard, therefore, to the similarity shown by John Wesley to his mother particularly, but in a real measure also to his father, it may be said that rarely has there appeared a man of such force of character and independence of thought who yet, in both career and character, was so much a home product. At Oxford, for the first time, he was able to put into independent practice a course of action for which he had been prepared alike by nature and upbringing, and this course of action was not limited either to the direct cultivation of his own soul or to the narrow circle of his college associates; at once it begins to look outward and to embrace the wretched, both young and old. This incipient social concern, it is significant, is constructive in kind if not very effective in result. In the education of the young and the relief of, as well as the religious ministration to, the

[10] Quoted: Bowen, op. cit., p. 98.
[11] See *Sermons*, I, Nos. 10 and 11; II, No. 45.
[12] Quoted: Eliza Clarke, *Susanna Wesley*, p. 16.

prisoners, it foreshadows the great social activities of Wesley's later years. His religion and his humanitarianism were interlocked from his Oxford days.

This humanitarianism, however, is different from what usually goes under that name because it is quite inseparable from Wesley's religious outlook. He did not give a man bread in order to save his soul, but it was primarily his desire to save the man's soul which made him concerned about his bodily needs. Very instructive is the 'Scheme of Self-Examination' used by the 'first Methodists in Oxford'. Under this, Mondays were devoted to an examination of one's love of man with six main questions, of which the first was: ' Have I been zealous to do, and active in doing good ? ' This is divided into fourteen sub-headings, some of which may be quoted as showing, on the one hand, Wesley's outlook very much that of his mother, and on the other, his subsequent organization and development of Methodism as already foreshadowed at Oxford. These are: ' Have I embraced every probable opportunity of doing good, and preventing, removing, or lessening evil ?—Have I pursued it with my might ?—Have I thought anything too dear to part with, to serve my neighbour ?—Have I, before I spoke to any, learned, as far as I could, his temper, way of thinking, past life, and peculiar hindrances, internal and external ? Fixt the point to be aimed at ? Then the means to it ?—Have I, in speaking, proposed the motives, then the difficulties, then balanced them, then exhorted him to consider both calmly and deeply, and to pray earnestly for help ?—Have I disputed upon any practical point, unless it was to be practised just then ?—Have I, when anyone asked advice, directed and exhorted him with all my power ? '[13] We may compare this with the

[13] *Arminian Magazine* (1781), IV.321–2.

'Right method of meeting Classes and Bands in the Methodist Societies', a scheme drawn up much later by Charles Perronet, one of Wesley's principal lieutenants, and a scheme Wesley approves and recommends. It says: 'The particular design of the Classes is: To know who continue members of the Society; to inspect their outward walking, to inquire into their inward state; to learn what are their trials; And how they fall by, or conquer them; . . . The particular design of the Bands is: To inquire whether . . . they aim at being *wholly devoted* to God; or would keep something back; . . . Whether they take up their cross daily; Resist the bent of nature; Oppose self-love in all its hidden forms; . . . Whether they are simple, open, free, and without reserve in speaking; And see it their duty and privilege so to be.'[14] Many years lie between these two schemes, and they are also separated by the great experience of Wesley's evangelical conversion, but they are in close relationship, and they both have close affinities with the upbringing in the Epworth Rectory.

EXPERIENCES WHILE IN GEORGIA

Wesley met James Edward Oglethorpe, the Governor of Georgia, in London. He had heard of him before, partly because Oglethorpe's projects for that colony were the subject of much general interest at the time, and also Samuel Wesley, his own father, had been interested, and had written these lines:

> *Yet, Britain, cease thy captives' woes to mourn,*
> *To break their chains, an Oglethorpe was born.*[15]

John Wesley was also influenced in regard to Georgia by Dr. Burton, one of that colony's trustees, and formerly of

[14] ibid., pp. 604–5.
[15] Quoted: Bowen, op. cit., p. 107.

Corpus Christi. To Dr. Burton, Wesley wrote at length his purpose and hopes in accepting work in Georgia: ' My chief motive,' he says, ' to which all the rest are subordinate, is the hope of saving my own soul. I hope to learn the true sense of the gospel of Christ by preaching it to the heathen. They have no comments to construe away the text; no vain philosophy to corrupt it; no luxurious, sensual, covetous, ambitious expounders to soften its unpleasing truths, to reconcile earthly-mindedness and faith, the Spirit of Christ and the spirit of the world. . . . By these, therefore, I hope to learn the purity of that faith which was once delivered to the saints; the genuine sense and full extent of those laws which none can understand who mind earthly things.

' A right faith will, I trust, by the mercy of God, open the way for a right practice; especially when most of those temptations are removed which here so easily beset me. Toward mortifying the desire of the flesh, the desire of sensual pleasures, it will be no small thing to be able, without fear of giving offence, to live on water and the fruits of the earth. This simplicity of food will, I trust, be a blessed means, both of preventing my seeking that happiness in meats and drinks which God designed should be found only in faith and love and joy in the Holy Ghost; and will assist me—especially where I see no woman but those which are almost of a different species from me— to attain such a purity of thought as suits a candidate for that state wherein they neither marry nor are given in marriage, but are as the angels of God in Heaven. . . .

' I then hope to know what it is to love my neighbour as myself, and to feel the powers of that second motive to visit the heathens, even the desire to impart to them what I have received—a saving knowledge of the gospel of Christ. But this I dare not think on yet. It is not for me, who have been a grievous sinner from my youth up, and am yet laden with foolish and hurtful desires, to expect God should work so great things by my hands.'[16]

With these two motives, Wesley set sail in October 1735 for Savannah, the capital of Georgia, accompanied by his brother Charles, Benjamin Ingham, and Charles Delamotte, all members of the Holy Club. He himself went in the capacity of clergyman, with a cure of souls; his brother as secretary to Oglethorpe; and with Delamotte as John's personal companion. Wesley had little to show for his time in Georgia except failure. He accomplished nothing in the way of evangelizing the Indians. It is true that in this he had little opportunity, for Oglethorpe wanted to canalize his activities into care for the colonists, and would not grant permission to go amongst the Indians, but was evasive when asked for it.

It would have been difficult for anyone, and impossible for such a man as John Wesley, with his strong sense of responsibility toward his neighbour and his keen interest in the manner of life of others, not to have received both a social and an economic education in a young society, such as that of Georgia, with its problems of cultivation, housing, public order, defence (against the French in the north and the Spaniards in the south rather than against the Indians), and problems regarding slavery, for although Georgia was not at that time a slave-owning colony, it was close to those which were. It is also significant, in the long tale of Wesley's connexion with poverty, that many of the colonists had gone to Georgia from debtors' prisons and the finances of the colony were always straitened.

In addition, John Wesley acted for a time in the capacity of secretary to Oglethorpe, instead of his brother Charles who had gone out in that appointment but had

[16] *Letters*, I.188-90.

proved utterly unsuited to it. This work brought John into touch with all the detail of the problems—governmental, financial, agricultural, social, and personal—with which the young colony was fraught.

His experiences in Georgia also brought him into relation with two problems, each of a mixed social-economic type, with which later on he was to have much to do, and about which he was to speak and write often. They were: slavery and spirits. Although there were, as pointed out above, no slaves in Georgia then, many people were agitating for their introduction, particularly because neighbouring colonies had slaves which meant that the settlers in Georgia felt themselves to be at an unfair disadvantage from an economic point of view. Again, many of these settlers were of a poor class, people who had failed under the less difficult conditions of England, and who felt that to sit back and watch the slaves do the laborious work was much to be preferred to having to do it for themselves. Not long after John Wesley's return to England, slavery was introduced into Georgia, during the time there of George Whitefield, a man who had not the objections to the practice, nor to the consumption of spirituous liquors, that Wesley had. It was rum that the people of Georgia sought to have imported, and this, too, was brought in soon after Wesley's departure. In England during most of the eighteenth century one of the greatest social problems was that of the consequences of the enormous consumption of gin. Both slavery and the consumption of spirits Wesley fought all his life, and his first contact with the former, and his earliest important contact with the problem of the latter, was in Georgia. While there he was also brought into close touch with the Moravians, a most important contact which we must now consider.

Chapter Two

Wesley's Evangelical Conversion and his Social Concern

ITS INWARDNESS, INDIVIDUALITY, AND OBJECTIVE CHARACTER

PRIOR to the 24th May 1738, the date of his 'evangelical conversion',[1] Wesley had been largely a frustrated man. He could neither settle at Oxford, Epworth, nor yet in Georgia. He felt himself always pursued by the necessity of living a yet more rigorous life, and none the less increasingly unsure as to his own salvation. Desiring most ardently to serve God, he counted himself more and more an unsatisfactory servant. Wishful of serving others, he could do little to affect the dour Fen folk of the Epworth parish, could gain few adherents at Oxford, and, as we have seen, failed completely in Georgia to evangelize the Indians or do more than raise bitter and prolonged opposition amongst the white settlers there. He returned to England early in 1738 as one who had not succeeded in the work he had gone out to do and had failed to achieve what he felt his religion both demanded and promised. His brother Charles had already returned, and also as a failure. It is interesting to note that Wesley did not seriously consider returning to Oxford and entering again on work at Lincoln College. His contact with the larger world, his experience of men and affairs recently gained, his sense of responsibility before God for others no

[1] This term is unsatisfactory, but is here employed because it is that by which many writers, and Methodist people generally, describe the experience it denotes. It is not true to say Wesley was unevangelical before or that until this event he was unconverted. (See pp. 16f. *infra*.)

less than for himself, all forbade that he should return to the old ways. He remained, therefore, in London, and put himself into contact with the Moravians, by whom he had already been considerably affected. By them he was urged to believe in salvation by faith, and faith alone, and to trust in Christ and in Christ crucified for him. This, he was told, he must not only accept as part of a creed, but must also *feel* with the complete conviction of an inner certainty. He did not know how he was to accept something with the certainty of an immediately felt experience when in fact he did not feel it, but the Moravian advice he received was that he need not wait for this to happen, but meanwhile should preach it. In short, he was not to preach faith because he felt it to be true, but he was to come to feel it to be true because he preached it. And in fact this is what happened.

All this appears plainly in a letter Wesley received from Peter Böhler a few days before his great experience. ' I love you greatly . . . praying . . . that you may taste, and then see, how exceedingly the Son of God has loved you, and loves you still; and that so you may continually trust in Him, and feel His life in yourself. Beware of the sin of unbelief; and if you have not conquered it yet, see that you conquer it this very day, through the blood of Jesus Christ. Delay not, I beseech you, to believe in *your* Jesus Christ; but so put Him in mind of His promises to poor sinners that He may not be able to refrain from doing for you what He hath done for so many others. . . . '[2] This letter followed advice, given a little before, that he should ' Preach faith *till* you have it; and then, *because* you have it, you *will* preach faith '.[3]

In a review of his life carefully made by Wesley at a

[2] *Journal*, I.461.
[3] ibid., p. 442.

later date he refers to the advice given him by Böhler and its influence on him: ' In my return to England, January 1738, being in imminent danger of death, and very uneasy on that account, I was strongly convinced that the cause of that uneasiness was unbelief; and that the gaining a true, living faith was the " one thing needful " for me. But still I fixed not this faith on its right object: I meant only faith in God, not faith in or through Christ. Again, I knew not that I was wholly void of this faith; but only thought I had not enough of it. So that when Peter Böhler, whom God prepared for me as soon as I came to London, affirmed of true faith in Christ (which is but one) that it had those two fruits inseparably attending it, " dominion over sin and constant peace from a sense of forgiveness ", I was quite amazed, and looked upon it as a new gospel.'[4] Later, he met Böhler again, and as a result of considerable discussion he arrived at the conclusion ' that this faith was the gift, the free gift of God; and that He would surely bestow it upon every soul who earnestly and perseveringly sought it '.[5]

Then, on the 24th May, something happened to him. He did not always interpret the experience in exactly the same way, or rather, as having exactly the same relationship to his previous religious life. It has been pointed out[6] that, after this experience, Wesley remarked that he who had gone to Georgia to convert others was unconverted himself, but later he adds a doubt: ' I am not sure of this.' While later still, and with greater insight, he says that at that time (i.e. in Georgia) he had ' the faith of a servant, not of a son '. The experience itself, whatever evaluation ought exactly to be given it, was not only

[4] ibid., p. 471.
[5] ibid., p. 472.
[6] W. H. Fitchett, *Wesley and his Century*, p. 128.

something intensely inward and personal, but also something objective. He believed certain things about God and the Person and Work of Christ and these he had believed for years, but his belief had been primarily an affair of the intellect, whereas now it became seated in the emotions. Before, he had believed that Christ had something which he hoped was also for him; now he trusted Christ for everything, here and hereafter. Before the 24th May, Wesley had anxiously been working out his salvation in fear and trembling, uncertain whether he really was saved or not. Thus, when asked by the Moravian, August Gottlieb Spangenberg, in Georgia, whether he knew himself saved or not, he hesitated and finally replied he hoped he was. Since the 24th May, he realized that he had no salvation now to work out, since thanks to what Christ had done, he really was saved. He now knew that in him the corpus of sin was destroyed, although he might still sin, never more would he do so habitually or with the consent of his mind. Thus, although the experience through which he had gone was so intensely individual, the character and training of the man, the experience in Georgia, and the objective aspect of that which he believed to have been done for him by Christ, all conspired to encourage him to look outward. And, in fact, we find him showing at once a social concern and interest even greater than before. It is true that there was immediately a keen testing-time as to the social side and bearing of the religious experience which was his, for the Moravians to whom he was so greatly indebted tended to sink into a subjective, emotional type of religion which was indifferent to the social challenge or was even antagonistic to it. Wesley's attachment to, and break from, the Moravians, was of great importance for his religious development and his social significance.

CONTACT AND CONTEST WITH THE MORAVIANS

On his way to Georgia, John Wesley went in a ship with a band of Moravians, amongst other passengers. During the voyage there was a dangerous gale, through which he made two discoveries, each of which made a profound impression on him. The first was that he could feel fear, and was afraid to die, and the second was that the Moravians gave no sign of fear, in marked contrast both to Wesley's inward state and to the outward condition of the other passengers. This was the beginning of an association with the Moravians in Georgia, London, and Germany, during the next two years, an association not confined to such individual contacts as those noted above, Böhler and Spangenberg, for example. In most of these contacts, Wesley was the learner, learning to give his emotions a place in his religion, at least equal to that of his intellect, a lesson extremely difficult for him to learn.

After his evangelical conversion, Wesley, now much enamoured of the Moravians, visited their headquarters in Germany, being particularly anxious to meet their leader, Count Zinzendorf, and to judge for himself the value of their social experiment at Herrnhut.[7] This is significant, for as soon as his new apprehension of religion had taken hold of him, he wanted to investigate a communal life in which were worked out from a religious point of view not only the details of worship, but a complete social order. Zinzendorf himself, a strange mixture of mystic and mountebank, did not attract Wesley, but the social experiment did. At Herrnhut, he observed with special interest the system of education, one which he was

[7] This experiment notwithstanding, the Moravians certainly tended to be indifferent to the social challenge, as stated on the previous page. Note Wesley's criticism referred to below (p. 20f.)

closely to follow a few years later in his own school at Kingswood.

On his return to London, he made common cause with the Moravians for a time, joining with their society in Fetter Lane. But this was not to last for long, because of their Antinomian tendencies. Wesley's divergence from them is brought out in his sermon on Sin in Believers, in which he says: 'Christ indeed cannot *reign* where sin *reigns*; neither will He *dwell* where any sin is *allowed*. But He *is* and *dwells* in the heart of every believer, who is *fighting against* all sin; although it be not yet purified, according to the purification of the sanctuary.

'It has been observed before, that the opposite doctrine —that there is no sin in believers—is quite new in the Church of Christ; that it was never heard of for seventeen hundred years; never till it was discovered by Count Zinzendorf. I do not remember to have seen the least intimation of it, either in any ancient or modern writer; unless perhaps in some of the wild, ranting Antinomians. And these likewise say and unsay, acknowledging there is sin *in their flesh*, although no *sin in their heart*. But whatever doctrine is *new* must be *wrong*; for the *old* religion is the only *true* one; and no doctrine can be right unless it is the very same "which was from the beginning".'[8]

Another point of grave difference between Wesley and the Moravians lay in their doctrine of 'stillness'. He records in the preface to the second part of his *Journal*[9] that 'about September 1739, while my brother and I were absent, certain men crept in among them (i.e. the members of the Society) unawares, greatly troubling and subverting their souls', teaching that a clean heart could not be obtained 'till you leave off using the means of

[8] *Sermons*, II.369–70.
[9] ibid. 430.

grace, so called; till you leave off running to church and sacrament, and praying, and singing, and reading either the Bible or any other book; for you cannot use things without trusting in them'. In the interests of grace they wished to abandon the means of grace. Chief amongst those bringing in this doctrine were the Moravians, Molther and Spangenberg. A long conflict took place, Wesley striving to combat this insidious doctrine, but finding its attraction for some too great for him to overcome. In the first ten days of November 1739 he struggled to make his view prevail, in London. He says: ' I observed every day more and more the advantage Satan had gained over us. Many of those who once knew in whom they had believed were thrown into idle reasonings, and thereby filled with doubts and fears, from which they now found no way to escape. Many were induced to deny the gift of God, and affirm they never had any faith at all, especially those who had fallen again into sin, and, of consequence, into darkness; and almost all these had left off the means of grace, saying they must now cease from their own works; they must now trust in Christ alone; they were poor sinners, and had nothing to do but to lie at His feet.'[10]

The differences between Wesley's views and those of the Moravians were by no means only theological, for Wesley was impressed by the social repercussions among the Moravians of their tenets. In a considered statement, written later (in 1750, in a letter), John Wesley details the points of difference between himself and the Moravians. In doing this, he says: ' I do not admire their confining their beneficence to the narrow bounds of their own society.'[11]

[10] *Journal*, II.315.
[11] ibid., III.504.

Referring to the effects of the preaching of Moravian views as he had observed them, in London and elsewhere, Wesley, in the same letter, says: 'This preaching has greatly impaired, if not destroyed, the love of their neighbour in many souls. They no longer burn with love to all mankind, with desire to do good to all.'[12]

After much effort and controversy, Wesley separated from the Moravians, withdrawing from their society in Fetter Lane, and commencing a new one at the Foundery. This separation is important for a proper understanding of the relation between his religious ideas and his social activity, because had he remained with the Moravians, sharing these doctrines of imputed, instead of inherent, righteousness, and of the uselessness, and even positive harm, of the 'means of grace', he could not have maintained the powerful ethical sense which was one of the main supports and impulses of his social work, nor could he have steeped himself in the Bible, with its strong reaction against social unrighteousness, its feeling for 'the under-dog', its plea for justice, and its constant witness to the responsibility of the individual before God for his possessions.

HIS ARMINIANISM

Wesley not only separated himself from the Moravians, but from the Calvinists, especially as represented by Whitefield. He firmly believed, and constantly preached, that in the love of God and the Work of Christ there was salvation available for all. In the eyes of God, everyone was of infinite value, His love and grace knowing no limit. The poorest, and socially most insignificant, could not only be saved, but could know his sins forgiven, a view which, significantly enough, gave great offence to some of those socially most distinguished. The Duchess of

[12] ibid., III.505.

Buckingham wrote with amazement and indignation to the Countess of Huntingdon, herself a Methodist, that she should tolerate for a moment such an outlook on the part of labourers, for the Duchess had the acumen to see that sooner or later those who were convinced that they were the objects of God's love and particular concern, would not remain indefinitely ' in that station to which it had pleased God to call them ', for a God who had direct dealings with them was likely to call them to some higher station. The truth was that such beliefs as these, which early Methodists were disseminating, would tend to break down that immobility of labour which was then as much desired in most parts of the country as it is often criticized now. These beliefs had in them a dynamic quality which would accord ill with the pre-Industrial Revolution static conception, both of society and of economic life.

Wesley, it is true, was far from encouraging those who came under his influence to be revolutionaries, or even to aspire to social advancement. Anything of that nature he would regard as sin and unhesitatingly make known his views. But the natural effects of such preaching could not be strait-jacketed and the man who passed through what was then a typical experience of emotional conversion, and who was encouraged thereafter to aim at perfection, would in most cases begin to rise economically and socially. Such a rise might result from either of two widely separated proximate causes, either through the experient himself feeling he was ' as good as ' anyone else who had received, or might receive, the grace of God, or through the added real dignity and greater incentive to hard and painstaking work to which his new status before God impelled him. In fact this latter cause often was found in operation. To persuade people of the importance, not of an elect few, but of every man in the sight of God, was a social factor of prime importance. Had Wesley been himself a revolutionary, instead of a man naturally conservative in outlook, the effect of his Arminianism might have caused great unrest, if no more. As it was, the effects of this teaching were canalized into tracks of individual improvement combined with concern for the souls and bodies of others.

We do not need to trace here the way in which Wesley had, against the natural effects of much of his early training and experience, come to be so deeply, and even passionately, convinced of God's love. We must, however, note that one result of this conviction was that his movement had an emotional element of great power. He refused to allow this emotion to be self-contained, still less to become, as was the case with some of the Moravians, erotic in form. On the other hand, he did not try to stifle it, having none of the cold outlook of many Calvinists. His own appeals were always to both head and heart, and this warm conception of God's concern for the poor as well as the rich, combined with the emotional possibilities, and even methods, not only of public evangelistic services, but of the band and class meetings so almost universal in eighteenth-century Methodism, were of great social significance. Because he refused to allow his converts to turn in upon themselves their emotional experience, he made them feel for others, developing in them not only social consciousness but social responsibility. Further, this emotionalism was a powerful outlet, or escape, from the depression of those masses whom even Wesley, with all his concern for them and appreciation of their possibilities, sometimes regarded as little better than beasts. The ugly little chapel which to the cultivated mind of today seems almost sacrilegious in its avoidance of anything suggesting beauty in worship, was a thing of real beauty to them. It represented colour, joy, strength, but it was more than a means of escaping from the hard realities of life. Undoubtedly it was to some extent that, but Wesley saw to it that this side should not receive over-emphasis. This he did by teaching that men must labour in whatever work they had to do as in the eyes of God, their work being an expression of their love to their Saviour. He also adopted the practical step of having, as far as possible, his weekday services either at 5 a.m., that is, before work, or in the evening after labour for the day was finished. There was no absenteeism caused through his preaching.

Wesley's emphasis on emotional conversion, and his reliance upon feeling-states as sure evidence of salvation, might have been expected to produce ethical chaos, and consequently great loss of social effectiveness, but for two limiting factors on which he also laid great stress. First, he emphasized good works as proceeding from the experience of salvation, and secondly, he instituted a rigorous system of discipline and oversight in regard to the private life, business concerns, and social activities of his adherents which left no room for doubt as to where a man's duty lay, nor as to whether he was doing it or not. It was expected that conversion should be followed by progress toward Christian perfection. Hence the social significance of the powerful emotional forces characteristic of early Methodism, for these forces were directed toward a personal perfection which was demonstrated and tested by good conduct toward others. Another element in the social significance of this emotional element is that the poor and uneducated could 'feel' even where they could not reason, and to this extent were on an equality with those of higher social and economic levels.

Even so, this emotional aspect ran to excess at times, and Wesley had, in part as the result of this excess, constantly to face charges of 'enthusiasm', and these he regarded with sufficient seriousness to answer carefully. The term 'enthusiasm' meant, in the eighteenth century, religious extravagance, especially any claim to have direct revelation by God's Holy Spirit. It is true it did not mean mere excitability, mere emotionalism, but a deeply felt religious emotion combined with the belief, and expectation, that God would have, and would maintain, direct touch with those whom His Son had saved. Wesley's Arminian outlook, combined with his own experience of evangelical conversion, implied that this kind of thing was only to be regarded as normal for all converts. In practice, it did sometimes lead to cases of enthusiasm, in the sense of the period, especially in the early days of the movement. These caused Wesley some hesitation at first, but gradually he was able to restrict these extravagances without damping down the real religious fervour. His own preaching on 'The Witness of the Spirit'[13] made possible expectations which, in the less balanced amongst his converts, would be likely to be 'enthusiastic'. However, Wesley devotes one of the 'Standard' sermons to this subject, as well as dealing with it in pamphlet form.

Thus, in his discourse on 'The Nature of Enthusiasm',[14] preached from the text, 'And Festus said with a loud voice, Paul, thou art beside thyself',[15] he defines the term 'enthusiasm', pointing out that many of those in the New Testament were men under the direct inspiration of God. He describes various manifestations of enthusiasm,

[13] See *Sermons*, II.341–59 compared with I.199–218.
[14] ibid., II.84–103.
[15] Acts 26^{24}.

and goes on to show that ' though there is a real influence of the Spirit of God, there is also an imaginary one; and many there are who mistake the one for the other. Many suppose themselves to be under that influence, when they are not, when it is far from them.' He ends by urging his hearers not to fall into any of the various forms of enthusiasm which he has outlined: ' Therefore constantly and carefully use all those means which He has appointed to be the ordinary channels of His grace. Use every means which either reason or Scripture recommends, as conducive (through the free love of God in Christ) either to the obtaining or increasing any of the gifts of God.'[16]

[16] *Sermons*, II.103.

Chapter Three
Social Implications of certain Doctrines Wesley commonly taught

CONVERSION AND ASSURANCE

IT HAD been difficult for John Wesley to be brought to the experience which he had on the evening of 24th May 1738. His upbringing, character, and ideals, were all against an emotional conversion. Nothing less than a complete *volte face* must accompany such an experience. It was not a new bias but a new life which became his that night, and with St. Paul, he would be ready to say: ' If any man be in Christ, he is a new creature: old things are passed away; behold, all things are become new.'[1] The very profundity of the change in him tended not only to authenticate the reality and validity of the experience so far as he was concerned, but to impress him with its high desirability for others. He does not reach the point of saying that a similar experience is absolutely necessary for every man, but he does hold that every man needs to be converted and expects that these conversions will be accompanied by experiences, especially emotional experiences, not dissimilar from those which he himself underwent.

The substance of Wesley's teaching on this subject is to be found in his *Standard Sermons*, Nos. 14, 15, and 39. The marks, he says, of those born of God, converted, are first: Faith, the content of which is confidence in God through what Christ has done combined with a total lack of confidence ' in the flesh ', in anything done or possessed, other than Christ Himself. Secondly, Hope, a living,

[1] 2 Corinthians 5^{17}.

assured hope of an eternal bliss. Thirdly, Love, the greatest of all, of which the necessary fruit is love towards one's neighbour, 'the hungering and thirsting to do good, in every possible kind, unto all men; the rejoicing to "spend and be spent" for them, for every child of man; not looking for any recompense in this world, but only in the resurrection of the just'.[2]

There are two points in Wesley's insistence upon conversion which are socially important, and none the less so because their effects are likely to be slow, and unperceived at the time by the person concerned. The first of these is his Pauline emphasis upon having no confidence in the flesh,[3] and that because this teaching strips from a man any reliance upon what he has done or upon what he possesses. Since his best efforts afford him no righteousness he can offer to God, no claim to heaven, still less can he offer his position or possessions as meriting any consideration whatsoever. Peasant and prince stand on the same level when it comes to life's most important experience. The wealthy man and the poor are in a similar plight; indeed, Wesley does not hesitate on the basis of his observation, to add that the poor man is in the better position for he has no wealth to encourage in him that pride which is enmity against God. In all this, Wesley was not preaching socialism—he was not even thinking of it. Nor was he desirous of giving the poor man 'a proper pride in himself'—far from it. None the less, such teaching could not fail to soften the hard outlines which so sharply distinguished the eighteenth-century 'manufacturer' or labourer from the man of substance, and even from the 'gentleman'. That this expectation was in fact realized is amply borne out in the

[2] *Sermons*, I.294.
[3] See Philippians 3[3].

SOCIAL IMPLICATIONS OF CERTAIN DOCTRINES 29

histories of converts of the Evangelical Revival. After their conversion, many showed a new determination and dignity in the presence of 'their betters', without any attempt or desire to claim a social equality with those of a higher class.

This teaching of Wesley on the impossibility of any person living that life of righteousness required of him, apart from his faith in the efficacy of the blood of Christ, strips from those who accept it any religious reliance upon externals, or upon good deeds done apart from faith. In particular, no reliance at all can be placed in wealth because it is uncertain, incapable of restoring the dearest things of life, and above all, completely useless to effect salvation: ' gold or silver. These are no more able to set thee *above the world*, than to set thee above the devil. ... Will thy riches reanimate the breathless clay ? ... But there is at hand a greater trouble than all these. Thou art to die! ... Now what help is there in your riches ? ... Can they deliver your soul, that it should not see death ? '[4] Such teaching was far from novel and can be paralleled in many a moralist and preacher. What was unusual, and perhaps unique, was the long period, over half a century, during which Wesley was saying this kind of thing, and the bluntness with which he said it, combined with his extraordinary power of touching men's consciences. His hearers, mostly men and women of little economic resource and of low social status, thus had wealth continually depreciated in their hearing, and so received a new perspective in these matters. At the same time, it should be noted, Wesley did not preach that men were called to remain static in that station in which they found themselves. On the contrary, by their honest work and frugality, men might become rich, and riches so won are

[4] *Sermons*, I.485–6.

nowhere denounced as sinful although constantly regarded as dangerous. The social importance of this teaching was not, therefore, that it was likely to make men content with their poverty so much as to make them inclined to value less highly positions of wealth and social distinction, by no means the same thing.

The second point of social importance in Wesley's teaching on the need for conversion is that he placed before men, instead of many classes and grades, two classes which were of far greater importance—the classes composed of the 'saved' and the 'unsaved' respectively. So the converted man did not feel that ordinary class-distinctions were ruled out, but they ceased to have the same significance because he was now so conscious that he was a member of that class of humanity known as the 'saved', opposed to which there was but one other, the 'unsaved'. A developed 'otherworldliness', while by no means implying a lack of interest in this world, must always diminish the importance previously attached to distinctions of rank, class, and wealth. The accident of birth might place a considerable gulf between rich and poor, but how much greater was the gulf between the 'once-born' and the 'twice-born'. The converted man belonged to a new 'upper class'.

The effects of this extreme valuation of a class, membership of which depended in no way upon wealth or status, were often observed in the bearing of converts. The case of John Haime, a soldier-preacher, illustrates this. He was actively preaching while on service with the Army in Flanders in 1739 and the years following. On being questioned by an officer as to the subject of his preaching, he replied: '" I preach against swearing, whoring, and drunkenness; and exhort men to repent of their sins, that they may not perish." He began swearing horribly, and said, if it were in his power, he would have me whipped to death. I told him, " Sir, you have a commission over men; but I have a commission from God to tell you, you must either repent of your sins or perish everlastingly ".'[5] Members of certain minor sects of to-day, who preach the same sort of message, and often in a similar manner to that of Wesley and his Preachers, show characteristics like those here outlined. Their attitude toward those who are socially and economically better placed than themselves is quite respectful but definitely coloured with a conscious superiority of class feeling, only the class in this case is that of the ' saved '. Of such are the Exclusive Brethren.

These social consequences of the preaching and experience of conversion were deepened and rendered more permanent by Wesley's emphasis upon the doctrine of Assurance. Like the rest of his teaching, this doctrine was not new, but fell upon the ears of his listeners with the novelty of long disuse. The essence of this doctrine, as he expounded it, is that the saved man receives an assurance within himself that his sins are forgiven him through his faith in what Christ has done for him, and that this assurance is occasioned by the Holy Spirit, and its consequence is a sense of joy and peace. In his own experience, Wesley records in his *Journal*[6] for 24th May 1738: ' An assurance was given me that He had taken away *my* sins, even *mine*, and saved *me* from the law of sin and death.' For years he held the view that this inner, spirit-given certainty was the possession of every converted man. On 25th January 1740 he writes: ' I never yet knew one soul thus saved without what you call " the

[5] *Lives of the Early Methodist Preachers*, quoted in Fitchett, *Wesley and his Century*, p. 237.

[6] *Journal*, I.476.

faith of assurance "; I mean a sure confidence that, by the merits of Christ, he was reconciled to the favour of God.'[7] Later, however, he modified his conviction that no person without this assurance could be converted, although he continued to expect that people would have this experience.

The importance of this doctrine of assurance lies in its claim that the saved person knows by an inner certainty that his sins are forgiven and he is at peace with God, and this immediate witness of the Spirit is supported by the witness of the conscience. Wesley insists on the importance of the joint character of this witness,[8] affording a conviction capable of sustaining a man not only through the depressing periods of his spiritual life, but especially giving him an inner joy and peace through the hard times of life, the ' common privilege of Christians fearing God and working righteousness '. Thus a spiritual compensation was provided for the social and economic inferiority of the converts to Methodism. This compensation was not in the nature of an opiate; it did not generally drug those who had to work very long hours, sometimes for very low wages, and often under unhealthy conditions of employment. No doubt it had that effect with some, but the way in which Wesley's converts tended to rise in the economic scale is disproof of any wide consequence of this sort. A man who had this assurance was a better workman, and often a better employer, than otherwise he would have been. This, indeed, he could hardly fail to be on psychological grounds, for whatever the theological validity of this experience (in the manner claimed by the early Methodist), there could be no doubt of its psychological effectiveness, for it marked almost the final step in the

[7] ibid., II.333-4.
[8] See *Sermons*, II.358.

resolution of competing mental states, and the resultant harmony was bound to lead to increased efficiency. A man who believed that the Holy Spirit gave him direct assurance that his immortal soul was saved, that a hitherto angry God now regarded him with favour and surrounded him with love, was delivered from many of those inhibitions and mental stresses which so greatly reduce efficiency.

Moreover, this doctrine of assurance, or rather, the experience of which the doctrine was the formulated expression, with its emphasis upon the directness of contact between the soul and the Spirit, puts still greater weight upon the importance of the class of saved persons as distinct from the unsaved. A man with such an experience might live socially poles apart from a lord, but he knew himself to be the recipient of a special concern, even a special revelation, from the Lord. This experience was an occasion for humility, not pride, but it none the less caused men to hold up their heads, with a new valuation of themselves, in wonderment and exultation. This attitude receives concrete expression in many of the hymns which John Wesley published, especially in those written by his brother Charles, and which were constantly sung by the converts.

HOLINESS AND PERFECTION

Wesley's call to men to be converted was supplemented by his emphasis upon the holiness taught in the Scriptures, as he understood it. This holiness, as he was careful to argue against those who urged the contrary, followed, and did not precede, justification, of which it was the proper consequence: ' Where there is no love of God, there is no holiness, and there is no love of God but from a sense of His loving us. . . . For it is not a saint but a sinner that is forgiven, and under the notion of a sinner. God justifieth not the godly, but the ungodly; not those that are holy already, but the unholy.'[9] God justified the man who has a living faith, by which faith he is born again, this great change being a work of God in the soul by the Holy Spirit, the result of which is a new creation in Christ Jesus, ' when it is " renewed after the image of God in righteousness and true holiness "; when the love of the world is changed into the love of God. . . . In a word, it is that change whereby the earthly, sensual, devilish mind is turned into the " mind which was in Christ Jesus ".'[10]

Wesley insisted that the principal reason for the new birth is that holiness may result, and holiness, Scriptural holiness, is not a catalogue of things to be done, but an inward experience by which the image of God is, as it were, stamped upon the heart, so that the heart for ever afterwards bears a new impress. This image, or impress, may be defined as the mind of Christ, and its characteristic expressions are thankful love to God and kindly love to man, and without this holiness, no man may see God.[11] The great experience of the New Birth cannot come without faith, saving faith, the whole trust of the heart as it goes out to Christ. But great as is the importance of this faith, it can never be a substitute for nor supersede the necessity of holiness.[12]

Again, great as is the consequence of this faith, Wesley teaches that it ' is only the handmaid of love '. This love is the beginning and end of everything, having primacy over all things. It is primarily love to God, occasioned

[9] *Sermons*, I.122 (on ' Justification by Faith ').

[10] ibid., II.234 (on ' The New Birth ').

[11] See ibid., p. 235.

[12] See *Sermons*, II.65 (on ' The Law Established through Faith ', Discourse 1).

by the contemplation of the love of God in Christ, and from this arises love to one's neighbour. Wesley does more than urge love to our neighbour, for he categorically states that such love cannot be avoided on the part of the man who loves God. The one is an inevitable result of the other, so that it becomes unthinkable that a man really loves God who does not truly love those with whom he has to do.[13] This love to one's neighbour is manifested negatively by doing him no harm, summed up in the observance of the Decalogue, but it does not stop at that. 'It continually incites us to do good, as we have time and opportunity; to do good, in every possible kind, and in every possible degree, to all men.'[14] Wesley would deny that a person living an anti-social life could be in the way of holiness, for good social relationships were a function of holiness. There can be no holiness without faith, and faith can neither be incurred nor maintained without good works.[15]

There is, of course, nothing original in such teaching, except perhaps in the plainness of language in which it was expressed. Many have preached the same without their preaching having any social effect except in the local and limited effect it may have had in softening personal relationships between individuals. In the case of Wesley, however, the matter is different. He was never content to point the moral, but must go on to indicate the fields in which the moral must be applied. To give at this point only one illustration, that of smuggling, he made abundantly clear the anti-social character of this very widespread practice, so that he might leave no one in doubt that a smuggler, or one who bought or sold

[13] cf. 1 John, especially 2^{10}f, 3^{14-18}, 4^{19-21}.
[14] *Sermons*, II.77, 81 (on 'The Law Established through Faith', Discourse 2).
[15] See ibid., II.457.

smuggled goods, was guilty of acting in an unloving way toward his neighbour, and therefore, toward his God. In other words one who profited by smuggling, directly or indirectly, denied his salvation, and so the fear and threat of hell fire was a sanction to deter a man from anti-social conduct. Wesley left no man in a state of comfortable assurance that he was eternally saved if he continued to profit by illegal importations. Thus were Wesley's religious ideas not only linked to his conception of good social conduct but used powerfully to reinforce it. Bluntly, he puts it thus: ' It is incumbent on all that are justified to be zealous of good works. And these are so necessary, that if a man willingly neglect them, he cannot reasonably expect that he shall ever be sanctified; he cannot grow in grace, . . . nay, he cannot retain the grace he has received; he cannot continue in faith, or in the favour of God.'[16] In other words, the saved man lives a socially useful life, and if he does not do so, he cannot remain in a state of salvation. The quality of a man's citizenship is one of the tests of his Christianity.

In this same passage, Wesley goes on to make clear what he means by good works. They are of two sorts, of which the first consists of religious devotions, study, and self-discipline. The second consists of ' all works of mercy ', including the relief of bodily necessities; visitation of prisoners and the afflicted; and the instruction of the ignorant. Such instruction was primarily for religious purposes, that is, to teach people the nature of Christianity, but in the pursuit of this it was necessary to teach the illiterate to read, in order that they might study the Scriptures, and so we find the Methodists keen supporters of eighteenth-century Sunday-schools, in which reading was the principal subject taught.

[16] *Sermons*, II.453-4.

Wesley was not content to preach the necessity of holiness, and to indicate particular ways in which it must be shown, and particular evils with which it would admit no compromise, but in addition he used the machinery of Methodist discipline to discover and punish (chiefly by excommunication from his Societies) such faults, and finally he would refuse, where an evil, such as smuggling, persisted, any more to come personally, a severe blow to those who were so much under the impress of his personality, and to whom he really was a 'father in God'. In short, Wesley's religious views and his social and economic teaching were never compartmentalized; both were aspects of his conception of the operation of divine grace, and both were enforced by his directness, persistency, and unique organization.

John Wesley was consistently emphatic upon the social character of the Christian religion and the social application of holiness. Against those who urged that holiness demanded, or implied, a life lived in solitary contemplation of God, he brusquely animadverted: 'Holy solitaries is a phrase no more consistent with the gospel than holy adulterers.' In his sermon written upon Matthew 5^{13-16} he interprets these words in a forthright social sense: 'In order fully to explain and enforce these important words, I shall endeavour to show, first, that Christianity is essentially a social religion; and that to turn it into a solitary one is to destroy it. Secondly, that to conceal this religion is impossible, as well as utterly contrary to the design of its Author.'[17] Similarly, and with a greater definition, when preaching upon Matthew 6^{1-15}, he goes out of his way to make clear not only the social obligations of the Christian religion, but the width of their scope: ' " That ye do not your alms ":

[17] ibid., I.381–2.

although this only is named, yet is every work of charity included, everything which we give, or speak, or do, whereby our neighbour may be profited; whereby another man may receive any advantage, either in his body or soul. The feeding the hungry, the clothing the naked, the entertaining or assisting the stranger, the visiting those that are sick or in prison, the comforting the afflicted, the instructing the ignorant . . . and if there be any other work of mercy, it is equally included in this direction.'[18]

The man who had been pursued painfully for so many years by the fear of losing salvation; the man who warned others of the dangers of hell fire and sought their emotional conversion; the man who plainly held up the other world as far more desirable (for the saved man) than this, regarding the death of a Christian as a triumph—this man it is who at the very point at which it might have been expected he would deal with the soul exclusively in its immediate relationship with God, yet does just the opposite, and labours to prove the social character of the Christian religion in general and its aspect of holiness in particular. In other words, his religious zeal and his social zeal were not finally separable. Nor, as we shall see, was this social enthusiasm merely an affair of 'ambulance work', concerned with the helping of those already in trouble; on the contrary, it aimed at the same time at preventing bad social conditions, it was concerned with the reformation as well as the reclamation of society. It has been pointed out that Wesley always made a point of preaching on 'The Communion of Saints' on All Saints' Day, a day for which he always showed an uncommon regard, and even when due allowance has been made for his unquestionable interest in the after

[18] ibid., I.426.

life, and his sense of the thinness of the intervening veil, it is difficult to resist the impression that there is a connexion between Wesley's own social sense and the social character of that doctrine.[19]

The social importance of Wesley's appeal to his followers to press on toward Christian perfection thus defined, to a state of sinlessness, is great because, as we have seen, he never regarded sin as a merely individual question. With all the importance he laid upon the salvation of the individual soul and with all the sense he had of each soul as standing alone before God, he always placed the individual in a social setting, and in practice regarded sins as primarily wrong thoughts, desires, and actions, between the person guilty of them and those with whom he had to deal. Wesley would not agree with the popular modern notion of a man sinning against himself. No better example of his attitude could be given than in the case already referred to, viz., smuggling, because here the harm done was indirect, through the loss occasioned to the State, and thereby to every citizen by the loss of State revenues. A man who can attack that so persistently and consistently, as Wesley did, clearly has given a strongly social connotation to the notion of holiness.

Long was the struggle Wesley had over the preaching of perfection. It was anything but popular among most Methodists, including his own brother, Charles, while outside the Methodist circle it was attacked, often violently. Among its more outstanding opponents was Toplady, the famous author of the hymn ' Rock of Ages ', who declared to Thomas Oliver, one of John Wesley's leading preachers: ' Certain I am, that your writers have

[19] See J. H. Overton, *John Wesley*, pp. 38–9. *Journal*, VIII.21: ' Being All Saints' Day, a day that I peculiarly love, I preached on Revelation 7^1; and we rejoiced with solemn joy.' (cf. ibid., III.381; IV.190; V.191, 236, 237n.)

no more title to arrogate meekness to themselves, than many of your preachers and perfectionists have to set up for a monopoly of holiness.'[20]

Membership of a Methodist Society, in fact, introduced the convert into much more than a religious society because every effort was made to make his religion a total affair. Hence such membership was a social experience in the widest sense, that is, it socialized on a religious basis the whole gamut of the convert's everyday experience. Holiness was not put into a separate compartment. On the contrary, it was intended to be a quality inherent in the whole of a man's interests. A Society member was not expected to have 'private' interests. As all his interests had a bearing upon salvation and as salvation was essentially social, that is, it had a social setting and social consequences, religion and life became coterminous. Few eighteenth-century Methodists would have understood the expression, 'Religion is what a man does with his solitariness', and fewer would have given it a second thought. Evidence of this social character of religious life is supplied by the titles of some of the Wesleys' hymns: Hymns of Physicians; for Women in Childbirth; for Journeys; for Visitation of a Friend; for a Child when Teething.[21]

---

[20] Augustus Toplady, *Works*, p. 841.

[21] Noted in J. Ernest Rattenbury, *Evangelical Doctrines of Charles Wesley's Hymns*, p. 57.

Chapter Four
Wesley's General Social and Economic Concern
STEWARDSHIP AND RESPONSIBILITY
REGARDING WEALTH AND TIME

THE GENERAL principle underlying Wesley's outlook on social and economic affairs was one of responsibility to God. He was possessed of a naturally inquiring mind, a lively interest in whatever came within his orbit, and a remarkable power of analysis and systematization; he was incapable of ignoring the conditions under which his converts in particular, and people in general, lived; and what he was incapable of ignoring he was unable to pass without comment supplied and remedy offered. Yet his sense of responsibility was not primarily one of a social character. In all his keen concern in social phenomena, Wesley's main motive was religious and not social, just as in all his philanthropy, he was an evangelist first and a philanthropist after. Whether he applied his mind to 'the scarcity of provisions' or spoke 'a word to a smuggler', he was giving expression to his own sense of responsibility before God, and encouraging others to admit and respond similarly for themselves.

He was a steward, and it is required of stewards that they be faithful. He well recognized the twofold nature of his stewardship. First, it embraced that which he had himself, his money, time, and talents. Secondly, it included his responsibility for the members of his Societies. The way in which he interpreted this second part of his stewardship made him not only a 'father in God' of the souls of his followers, but a trustee before God of the way in which they used those things of which they were possessed. One cannot, therefore, draw a clear line of demarcation between Wesley's religious teaching and his social and economic views, for the latter were regarded by him as particular illustrations of the former. In other words, for John Wesley, economic laws could have no authority except they were congruous with religious interests. This is not to say that he pronounced upon social and economic questions without studying them empirically. On the contrary, his approach was inductive up to a considerable point, and he spoke as one who had opportunities of observing contemporary facts, greater than those of any other person in the realm. But whatever conclusions he drew as to actual prevailing conditions he would apply them on a basis of responsible stewardship before God. The last word always lay with God, in social and economic matters as in other things.

It is important at every stage to remember that Wesley's sense of responsibility was definitely religious. He was convinced that he would ultimately have to face the Great Judge to account for those to whom (he was sure) he was sent, and accordingly he must at all times faithfully speak and act for God. This starting-point in his attitude of mind is well brought out in his sermon on ' Christian Perfection '.[1] He refers at the beginning to the dislike which men had to the preaching of Christian Perfection, but says: ' Whatsoever God hath spoken, that will we speak, whether men will hear, or whether they will forbear; knowing, that then alone can any minister of Christ be " pure from the blood of all men ", when he hath " not shunned to declare unto them all the counsel of God ".'[2] This is more than an illustration of Wesley's

[1] *Sermons*, II.150–74.
[2] ibid., p. 151.

moral courage; it is also an enunciation of a basic principle which governed all his thinking, namely, that he was responsible at every point to God and this responsibility included others as well as the things he might have called his own.

Thus Wesley's sense of religious responsibility was both general and special. General because he was sure he would have finally to account to the Great Judge for everything 'done in the body'. Special in two ways: first, through his particular sensitiveness to the duty of the right use of money and time, and secondly, because he was conscious, with St. Paul, that 'a dispensation of the Gospel' had been committed unto him, and one which demanded that he should declare the 'whole counsel of God'. This sensitiveness to the moral claims set up by the possession of any degree of wealth, and of the use of time, he shared with many moralists of many periods, and notably with those belonging to, or following from, the Puritan tradition. It may also be conjectured, however, that these views were rendered more powerful in their appeal through his first-hand experience at home, and later at Oxford, of the consequences which might follow a wrongful use both of money and time. His father had ensured the poverty of his family by careless and almost unprincipled waste of resources, while his use of time was open to criticism. The older Wesley was by no means lazy, but he had little idea of the relative importance of claims upon him; whenever his literary interests were involved, he was incapable of imagining any better use of his time. His *magnum opus*, on Job, demanded, and got without stint, the equivalent of years of his life, while other literary works also took up a considerable part of his time, time which might otherwise have been available for other occupations of his calling.

Samuel Wesley was not only an object lesson to his son on how not to look after money and how not to spend time, but also on the dangers of a false valuation of himself and his abilities. This may in part account for one remarkable aspect of John Wesley's character. Although he was autocratic in his direction of his concerns, and of the lives of those with whom he had to do, yet he welcomed eagerly and almost pathetically, the criticism, even the biting criticism of others. ' Every man in my band is my monitor, and I his; else I know no use of our being in band.'[3] True, he might discard the criticism as unjustified and therefore of no value, and often did so, but not before he had turned it over in his mind, and it is a remarkable fact that he seldom if ever took umbrage at it. Here we have a moralist and a spiritual director who really considered a favour to have been shown him by any who would sit in judgement upon him. Nothing could give more convincing evidence of his real sense of responsibility. A weak man may welcome criticism because he is afraid of responsibility, but in this case, a man of the strongest will welcomes criticism because he is sensible of his obligations and determined to discharge them to the utmost of his ability.

The importance of Wesley's strong sense of stewardship lay in its effects, through his life and teaching, and the discipline which he imposed upon the Methodist Societies. Indeed, whenever the Christian religion, and the Jewish religion out of which it sprang, are taken seriously, they are apt to inculcate a sense of trusteeship, both in respect of what is possessed materially, as regards wealth, and immaterially as regards time and power. ' The earth is the Lord's, and the fulness thereof' provides a theological

[3] Written in a letter to James Hutton, dated 26th November 1738—*Letters*, I.272.

GENERAL SOCIAL AND ECONOMIC CONCERN 45

basis for the believer to dispossess himself of any claim to absolute ownership of property and of any vagueness of attitude toward any form of opportunity. Men so convinced may be, as John Wesley was, social reformers, or at least, men of great influence on the social outlook of their times, but if they are so it is because of their religious interest and the sanctions which arise therefrom.

Wesley was well aware that his own conception of stewardship evoked little more than lip-service from many of his followers, if indeed it did so much as that, but this only added to the force with which he proclaims his view, and the strictness with which he employed his discipline thereto. His warnings to his rich hearers[4] indicate this clearness of vision as does also his statement that Satan, in his efforts to wreck Methodism, first raised up against it Calvinism, then Antinomianism, and finally 'many Methodists grew rich, and thereby lovers of the present world'.[5] In a sermon on 1 Timothy 6[9] Wesley deals with such men. He says: ' O ye Methodists, hear the word of the Lord! I have a message from God to all men; but to *you* above all. For above forty years I have been a servant to you. . . . I have testified to you the very same thing, from the first day even until now. But *who hath believed our report?* I fear not many rich, I fear there is need to apply to some of you those terrible words of the Apostle, *Go to now, ye rich men! Weep and howl for the miseries which shall come upon you. Your gold and silver is cankered, and the rust of them shall witness against you, and shall eat your flesh, as it were fire.* Certainly it will, unless ye both save all you can, and give all you can. But who of you hath considered this, since you first heard the will of the Lord concerning

---

[4] E.g. *Sermons*, II.486. (See also Sugden's Note on Sermon 44, ibid., p. 310.)

[5] *Minutes of Conference*, 1812 edition, p. 50.

it? Who is now determined to consider and practise it? By the grace of God begin to-day!'[6] On the other hand, it must be borne in mind that Methodists who became rich did not necessarily become 'lovers of the present world', particularly if they were engaged in trade, because the possibilities of the expansion of trade called for more and more capital which meant, as a rule in those days, returning to the business money saved from it. A man might, it is true, become too much absorbed in the expansion of his business, but even where this occurred the results were unlikely to be so deadening to his religious life as would have been the case if his expenditure on consumers' goods and services connected with pleasure had increased.

'Labour is not merely an economic means: it is a spiritual end. Covetousness, if a danger to the soul, is a less formidable menace than sloth. . . . So far from there being an inevitable conflict between money making and piety, they are natural allies, for the virtues incumbent on the elect—diligence, thrift, sobriety, prudence—are the most reliable passports to commercial prosperity.'[7] This quotation has to do with Calvinism, and however much Wesley might differ from Calvinism in matters of doctrine and religious outlook, he shared its temper in large measure in regard to economic affairs. One of his preachers, Thomas Taylor, noted significantly, about 1780 at York: 'There is but little trade in any part of the Circuit; and when there is little trade, there is seldom much increase in religion'.[8] However numerous writers on various aspects of this duty of regarding all things, and

[6] *Arminian Magazine* (1781), p. 76.

[7] Max Weber, *The Protestant Ethic and the Spirit of Capitalism*, foreword by R. H. Tawney, p. 3.

[8] *Lives of the Early Methodist Preachers*, V.5, p. 56.

particularly wealth and time, as a stewardship held from God, might be (and they were many), Wesley has a great importance in this respect because of the effectiveness with which he propagated his views, by sermons, writings, and precept, and, as we shall see later, by the remarkable discipline he exercised over his preachers and followers generally.

CALLING, OR VOCATION

One aspect of the doctrine of the Priesthood of all Believers is its tendency to equate the religious value of occupations, unless an occupation is inherently undesirable, i.e. one which militates against a divine law, such as the occupation of a burglar. If any Christian man can, and indeed ought to, regard himself as a Christian priest, living a holy life, that is, one ' separate from the world ', it follows that one rightful occupation is as much a vocation as another. And when a man's work is so regarded it becomes an expression of his religion. This expression is more than a matter of practising honesty in business, although of course it includes that. Further, it is more than a question of the right use of money and time. It is a matter of faith as well as morals. One should not therefore dismiss as cant or blind pietism the statements of those who averred that God would look after the good man's business. God was felt to be implicated in the success of His servants, much in the same way as, in the Old Testament, we find it stated that the good prosper and the evil suffer. If a Methodist tradesman failed in business, some members of the Society might be expected to take a line similar to that of Job's friends, namely, that however good he might have appeared to be, there must have been something wrong with his life somewhere, some form of secret sin. The importance of such an attitude is twofold: it tended to make Methodists, and others of similar views, work all the harder to be successful, and, on the other hand, supplied a sanction for a higher standard of conduct, both for business activities and personal life.

John Wesley regarded wealth as anything but an evil in itself. On the contrary, he frequently urged that it could be an instrument of very great good.[9] Hence, on this score also, the choice of a calling was most important. This laid a big responsibility on parents for they were expected to start their sons out in life on such lines that through their work they might be able to express their religion. This implied that the work chosen should not be such as to lessen the chances of the salvation of the youth's soul, and also that through it God's glory might be enhanced. Of course, such conscious choosing after a weighing-up of pros and cons was not possible for all. Most Methodists, being poor men, must put their sons, and often their daughters, to work where they could, probably at the staple trade of the district. But this practical limitation did not absolve them from the duty of ensuring that no youth was put to work under conditions likely to do harm to his soul. If a girl was put into domestic service, the commonest occupation open, taking the country as a whole, she was none the less to regard it as her vocation, and her employer should act in a reciprocal spirit toward her.

OTHERWORLDLINESS AND RESIGNATION

Wesley's primary concern, both for himself and others, was the salvation of the soul. Yet he did not, on this account, deny the importance of the things which belonged to the secular interests and activities of people. Nor did

[9] Illustrations of this view from his teaching will be found in Chap. 6, pp. 110–111, *infra*.

he take a pessimistic view of them. His attitude was not that it was an unfortunate fact that we should have bodies with needs to be met, and a social and economic life to be lived. On the contrary, he held that proper attention to bodily needs, proper discharge of social responsibilities, were religious acts. If a man were responsible to God for his use of possessions and time, then clearly possessions and activities were not in themselves evil. If one's work were regarded as a vocation from God, worldly activities could be, and should be, instrumental to the Christian life, not because they could put a man right before God, for justification is by faith alone, but because they provided a proper field for the exercise of the life of faith.

This teaching, however, was not enough, for very few would be able to resist the downward pull of these worldly interests for long, unless fortified in some other direction. There is always the danger for a man busy with affairs that he should become absorbed in them, especially when he is bidden, as a religious duty, to employ fully every minute. Absorption in one's calling may become absorption by one's calling. It is the old problem of living in the world without being of the world; only in the case of the Methodist Societies this problem was particularly acute just because of the power with which Wesley made his appeal to the sense of responsibility, and the authority of the discipline by which the appeal was enforced. Hence it came about that Wesley preached incessantly on the danger of worldliness and the corresponding need for otherworldliness. Perhaps he never quite resolved the paradox of insisting on great activity in worldly matters while preaching otherworldliness, or if he resolved it in his own mind he could not always resolve it in the minds of others. It is significant that a note of bitterness would sometimes creep into his references to well-to-do Methodists. Thus in writing to Dorothy Furley (May 1757) he speaks of the need for a deep desire to become altogether Christ-like, to have a ' strong thirst after His whole image. Such I take most of the leaders of bands to be; and such are many of the poor in the Society, but extremely few of the rich or honourable Methodists are of that number'.[10] In 1763, at Bristol, Wesley ' gave our brethren a solemn caution not to " love the world, neither the things of the world ". This will be their grand danger; as they are industrious and frugal, they must needs increase in goods. This appears already. In London, Bristol, and most other trading towns, those who are in business have increased in substance sevenfold, some of them twenty, yea, an hundredfold. What need, then, have these of the strongest warnings, lest they be entangled therein, and perish? '[11] The following year, at Stockport, he gives another ' solemn warning ', for, he states: ' Riches swiftly increase on many Methodists, so called. What but the mighty power of God can hinder their setting their hearts upon them ? And if so, the life of God vanishes away.'[12] At London, in 1767, Wesley ' was desired to preach a funeral sermon for William Osgood. He came to London near thirty years ago, and, from nothing, increased more and more, till he was worth several thousand pounds. He was a good man, and died in peace. Nevertheless, I believe his money was a great clog to him, and kept him in a poor, low state all his days, making no such advance as he might have done, either in holiness or happiness '.[13] To take but one other illustration of this consistent view

[10] *Letters*, III.214.
[11] *Journal*, V.30–1.
[12] ibid., pp. 82–3.
[13] ibid., p. 245.

which Wesley held—at Macclesfield, as an old man now, he preaches in 1787. There, he 'found a people still alive to God, in spite of swiftly increasing riches. If they continue so, it will be the only instance I have known, in above half a century. I warned them in the strongest terms I could, and believe some of them had ears to hear.'[14]

It is not surprising to find that the first sermon Wesley preached after his ordination was from the text: ' But seek ye first the kingdom of God, and His righteousness; and all these things shall be added unto you,'[15] and that the same sermon, or one very like it, was preached in areas as widely separated as Oxfordshire, London, Ireland, Manchester, Bath, and Bristol. It was preached at Kingswood thirty-six years after its first pronouncement, and appears in the *Standard Sermons*[16] in the list on the Sermon on the Mount. The preacher emphasizes the impossibility of a man serving God and wealth (Mammon). He goes on to define the service of God as believing in Him (which implies trusting Him for strength and happiness), and as having ' an eye to Him in all things '. The service of God is further defined as loving Him, and still further as imitating and obeying Him. Contrariwise, Wesley then defines the service of Mammon as trusting in it, finding one's happiness in it. ' And if we do this, we cannot but make the world our end; the ultimate end, if not of all, at least of many, of our undertakings, many of our actions and designs; in which we shall aim only at an increase of wealth, at the obtaining pleasure or praise, at the gaining a larger measure of temporal things, without any reference to things eternal.'[17]

[14] ibid., VII.256.
[15] Matthew 6^{33}.
[16] *Sermons*, I.495-515.
[17] ibid., p. 500.

And this service of Mammon implies love of the world, imitating and obeying the world. He makes clear what is exactly in his mind in the idea of obeying the world: it means 'to be in the fashion; to follow a multitude; to do like the rest of our neighbours: that is, to do the will of the flesh and the mind, to gratify our appetites and inclinations; to sacrifice to ourselves; aim at our own ease and pleasure. . . .'[18]

As it is thus seen to be impossible to serve both God and Mammon, 'thou shalt seek nothing in earth or heaven but Him'. Then Wesley immediately goes on to point out that this does not mean, as on the surface it might appear to do, that business is of no consequence. On the contrary, the Christian must not be slothful, which indeed he will hate to be as much as he will hate to be drunken, or as to be guilty of adultery. No, rather it is God's will that everyone should be self-supporting, for himself and his household, and should keep out of debt. To do this a man must often give much earnest thought. He must plan his business ventures before he enters upon them and, from time to time, he ought carefully to consider the next steps to be taken in his economic activities, and in accordance with his plans he must make preparation beforehand to implement what he proposes to do. Wesley later qualifies this injunction to business-prevision by saying that one ought not to look too far ahead: 'Do not trouble yourself now, with thinking what you shall do at a season which is yet afar off. Perhaps that season will never come; or it will be no concern of yours; before then you will have passed through all the waves, and be landed in eternity.'[19] Still more, he urges men never to allow the real need for concern in business affairs to

[18] ibid., p. 501.
[19] ibid., p. 509.

divert them from the present necessity of attending to religious and other duties lying to hand. Further, he condemns men whose present conduct they themselves acknowledge to be wrong, but upon the plea that the duty of providing for self and family make it necessary. This, Wesley asserts, is very common. He does not mention the view sometimes put forward, that it is impossible for a man to be honest in business, but it would have been apposite to his illustrations and argument. His reply to that sort of thing is clear cut: ' Many, if we exhort them to keep a conscience void of offence, to abstain from what they are convinced is evil, do not scruple to reply: " How then must we live ? Must we not take care of ourselves and of our families ? " And this they imagine to be a sufficient reason for continuing in known, wilful sin. They say, and perhaps think, they would serve God now, were it not that they should, by-and-by, lose their bread. They would prepare for eternity; but they are afraid of wanting the necessaries of life. So they serve the devil for a morsel of bread; they rush into hell for fear of want; they throw away their poor souls, lest they should, some time or other, fall short of what is needful for their bodies ! '[20]

This primacy of place accorded to affairs of the world Wesley opposes as something induced not only by fear of future want but, more positively, by desire for material satisfactions. Whereas, he says, men bear the stamp of Satan in that they are guilty of self-will, they go even beyond Satan himself ' into an idolatry whereof he is not guilty: I mean, love of the world; which is now as natural to every man, as to love his own will '.[21] This he explains to be the love of the things made by the Creator

[20] ibid., p. 510.
[21] ibid., II.219.

rather than the Creator Himself. Nor will he allow as genuine the plea of many, especially of the educated classes, that they really despise the pleasures of the senses. This, he dismisses as mere affectation. Then he places on the same level those pleasures which are not material but the result of the imagination, his principal objection to them being that men are always desiring something new:

> *The hoary fool, who many days*
>   *Has struggled with continued sorrow,*
> *Renews his hope, and fondly lays*
>   *The desperate bet upon to-morrow !*
>
> *To-morrow comes ! 'Tis noon ! 'Tis night !*
>   *This day, like all the former, flies :*
> *Yet on he goes, to seek delight*
>   *To-morrow, till to-night he dies !* [22]

Wesley then adds: ' A third symptom of this fatal disease —the love of the world, which is so deeply rooted in our nature—is " the pride of life "; the desire of praise, of the honour that cometh of men.' This desire for praise and honour he denounces as very widespread, even amongst many of those who are commonly regarded as outstanding Christians.

All this worldliness is due, Wesley maintains, to the great fact of the total corruption of human nature, of original sin; and so radical a state of disease needs a correspondingly radical cure. ' By repentance and lowliness of heart, the deadly disease of pride is healed; that of self-will by resignation, a meek and thankful

[22] ibid., p. 221. (These verses Wesley quotes from Prior's ' Lines to the Hon. Charles Montague '.)

GENERAL SOCIAL AND ECONOMIC CONCERN 55

submission to the will of God; and for the love of the world in all its branches, the love of God is the sovereign remedy. Now, this is properly religion: " faith " thus " working by love ": working the genuine meek humility, entire deadness to the world, with a loving, thankful acquiescence in, and conformity to, the whole will and word of God.'[23]

So Wesley's teaching on otherworldliness is based upon two religious ideas. First, that everything in the world is not only from God, but always belongs to Him. Secondly, that man is by nature universally corrupt, a state from which he can be redeemed only by a total work of God in the soul, resulting not in a contempt for the world, but in a deadness to it. This deadness is possible only so long as the man is alive to God, and such life depends upon his continual resignation to the will of God. It is important to notice that this resignation is positive and not negative, and in no way implies contempt for, or indifference to, the everyday life of the world. Deadness to the world does not mean indifference to it, but indifference to its rewards and penalties, whether material in the form of increased or diminished wealth, or immaterial in the form of praise or censure. Indeed, the more truly a man's will is resigned to God, the more readily will he do the will of God, and the sphere of that Divine activity through him must be in this world seeing he is an embodied spirit. Consequently, it may be expected that a man who adopts Wesley's standpoint, and comes into the relation of utter dependence upon God, will be ready to be led of God to works of social and economic value. In fact it was notably so with Wesley himself, for his otherworldliness was one of the springs of his social and religious activity. In conversing with a lady who expressed her sorrow at his leaving his friends

[23] ibid., p. 224.

'to lead this vagabond life', he replied: 'Why, indeed, it is not pleasing to flesh and blood; and I would not do it if I did not believe there was another world.'[24] Thus his otherworldliness became a religious motive for work in this world, and his resignation to the will of God made him, not a fatalist, but a reformer.

[24] *Journal*, IV.13.

Chapter Five
Wesley's Concern with Certain Social Questions
SMUGGLING AND LIQUOR

THE EIGHTEENTH-CENTURY economic evil of smuggling and the social evil of widespread drinking of spirits were bound up together. The prevalence of these twin evils was inescapable and was certainly not overlooked by Wesley. He was, of course, far from unique in fighting them. The Government throughout the century was fighting a protracted battle with the smuggling interests, while moralists, reformers, and magistrates, were frequently crying out against the consequences of the consumption of spirituous liquors. There are no figures in existence to show the annual consumption of liquor in the Wesley period. Statistics were in those days often suspect, but apart from this, owing to illicit distilling and smuggling no accurate figures are to be expected. We can, however, get some idea of the trend of consumption from the figures of spirits distilled and reported:[1]

Year	Spirits distilled (gallons)	Year	Spirits distilled (gallons)
1684	527,492	1744	6,627,494
1694	810,096	1754	5,051,002
1704	1,375,496	1764	2,219,731
1714	1,950,827	1774	2,009,994
1724	3,563,625	1784	1,337,912
1734	6,074,562	1794	4,594,793

[1] See *First Report of Commissioners of Inland Revenue* (1857), Appendix 19, quoted in E. D. Bebb, *Nonconformity and Social and Economic Life, 1660–1800*, p. 146. The returns commence in 1684. On the also large consumption of beer, see Webb, *The History of Liquor Licensing in England*, p. 18; and *Economic History Supplement to the Economic Journal* (May 1927), p. 271–2.

Prior to the outbreak of war with France in 1688, when the importation of spirits was forbidden, the supply had come partly from France and partly from production at home, confined to Royal patentees. In 1690 monopoly conditions of production ceased and anyone might distil on payment of a low excise duty, retailers of spirits requiring no licence. The result of this was the very great increase of 'dram shops' for the sale of spirits at very low prices. For a person to become 'drunk for a penny and dead drunk for twopence' became quite a simple affair, and no less common than simple. There was no sanction of public opinion against drunkenness nor against smuggling. The governmental authorities struggled to a limited extent against drunkenness and to a considerable, but mostly ineffective extent, against smuggling. A series of Acts was passed during the century, of which a large number were of little value, but by the end of the eighteenth century they had brought under the control of the Justices the retail sale of all intoxicating liquors, for consumption on the premises.[2]

Although the mortality from the high degree of spirit-drinking was serious, and its evil gradually became more noticeable, it was a long while before those who wished to see its curtailment could make much headway. Foremost amongst these, not only in the strength of his attitude, but in the degree of success he obtained, was John Wesley. Although not a teetotaller himself, he set his face against the drinking of spirits, not only in regard to his personal example, but in the similar example he demanded from his preachers, and expected from the members of his Societies. He was not only against the consumption but also against the trade in liquor, as

[2] See *Royal Commission on Licensing (England and Wales)* (1929–1931), pp. 264–9.

represented by spirits. In the case of beer of low specific gravity, however, his attitude was different; in fact, he advised his preachers to drink it rather than tea, while he himself experimented with brewing ale in London, trying one barrel without hops and another with.[3]

Against the use of, and trade in, spirits, Wesley preached and wrote and also exercised the Methodist discipline. In his famous sermon on the 'Use of Money' he categorically states that no Christian can take part in any commercial operations which may cause harm to the bodies of others, and specifically mentions trafficking in liquor.[4] In characteristic language, he writes to Richard Steel in 1769: 'Touch no dram. It is liquid fire. It is a sure though slow poison. It saps the very springs of life.'[5] He adds: 'In Ireland, above all countries in the world, I would sacredly abstain from this, because the evil is so general.'

The question was dealt with at the annual Methodist Conference of 1765, in the usual form of question and answer: '*Q.* How shall we cure them (our people) of drinking drams? *A.* 1. Let no preacher drink any, on any pretence. 2. Strongly dissuade our people from it. 3. Answer their pretences; particularly those of curing the colic, and helping digestion.'[6] By these quotations it will be seen not only that Wesley had set himself in opposition to both the trade in, and consumption of, spirits, but that he had a definite plan of campaign in which example (that of himself and his preachers) and instruction in sermon and letter was backed by rule and discipline throughout the Societies. He did not, it is true,

[3] He recounts this in a long letter to the *Bristol Gazette*, written in 1789, on the question of the use of hops in brewing (see *Letters*, VIII.166).
[4] *Sermons*, II.317–18.
[5] *Letters*, V.134; Wesley, *Primitive Physic*, p. 12, Preface.
[6] *Minutes of Conference*, 1765 (1812 Edn., I.51–2).

make abstention a *sine qua non* of membership, but he approached that point. In his campaign against smuggling, we shall now note that he passed this point, and it is not difficult to see why; for as the law, backed by the preventive service, gradually, and with lapses, made promiscuous and dangerous drinking more difficult, so the rewards of successful smuggling became higher. Smuggling lay, therefore, at the root of much of the social evil of spirit consumption, while in addition it had economic and moral objections of its own by operating against the public income through taxation and by the whole system of lying, thieving, and chicanery to which it gave rise. Wesley saw that great as were the evils of 'dram drinking' those connected with smuggling were greater, and therefore he reacted against it the more vigorously.

Although spirits were the principal articles of the smuggling traffic, they were not the only ones, and therefore more people were affected. People who would not drink spirits might buy other 'uncustomed' articles, and in fact they did so widely. Nor was this confined to the less respectable members of society, for public opinion generally did not regard it as reprehensible. A country parson, for instance, might have no qualms of conscience at getting something cheaper in this way, as witness Parson Woodforde's naïve admissions in his diary: '1778, Feb. 23. To my smuggler Andrews for a Tub of Gin . . . £1. 5. 0. 1780, May 17. I did not got to bed until after twelve at night, as I expected Richard Andrews the honest smuggler with some Gin.'[7]

---

[7] *The Diary of a Country Parson*, by the Rev. James Woodforde (1758–1781). Eighteenth-century smuggling was in some ways the opposite of mid-twentieth-century 'black market', for it meant the sale of goods at less than the market price, and increased the total volume of goods current in the country.

One of the most widely distributed tracts of Wesley was *A Word to a Smuggler*, first published in 1767. It was sold and otherwise distributed by thousands. As his preachers travelled over the country on horseback, their saddlebags carried their load of tracts, and amongst them this one had a foremost place. In it Wesley deals specifically with the two questions regarding smuggling which presented the greatest difficulty. These questions were: How can a person, not dealing at first hand with a smuggling organization, know that goods offered for sale have in fact been smuggled? and, What is there morally wrong in the practice? To the first question, he answered plainly, ' Did not he that sold it tell you it was? If he sold it under the common price (i.e. the market price), he did. The naming the price was telling you, " This is run ".' To the second question, he replied, ' Open smuggling (such as was common a few years ago, on the southern coasts especially) is robbing on the highway. . . . Private smuggling is just the same with picking of pockets. . . . It is, in effect, not only robbing the King, but robbing every honest man in the nation. For the more the King's duties are diminished, the more the taxes must be increased '.[8]

In a Pastoral Letter to the Bristol Society, Wesley wrote in 1764: ' Defraud not the King any more than your fellow subject. Never think of being religious unless you are honest.'[9] Also at Bristol, in 1778, Wesley spent three days examining the Classes, principally to discover ' whether there was any truth in the assertion that above a hundred in our society were concerned in unlawful distilling. The result was that I found two persons, and no more, that were concerned therein '.[10] And sixteen

[8] *Works*, XI.170 and 167.

[9] *Letters*, IV.272.

years later, to one of the preachers, he wrote: 'We will have no smugglers in our Societies.'[11] This preacher was William Tunney, in Cornwall East. One of Wesley's early converts was a young smuggler, a man who started by disturbing a meeting, in London in 1740, remained, and presently 'came and declared before us all that he was a smuggler, then going on that work; as his disguise, and the great bag he had with him, showed. But, he said, he must never do this more, for he was now resolved to have the Lord for his God'.[12]

Cornwall was not only one of the principal areas in which smuggling was rife but was also notorious for the somewhat analagous crime of the plundering of wrecked vessels, of which mention may be made here, for this did not escape Wesley's notice. In 1776, he inquires, while in Cornwall, if this scandal still existed, and was informed: 'As much as ever; only the Methodists will have nothing to do with it.'[13]

SLAVERY

The abolition of slavery in the British Empire belongs to the early nineteenth century, but the long fight of the Abolitionists, especially in respect of the education of public opinion, largely belongs to the eighteenth century. Before Wesley's day there was a number who not only thought slavery a wrong institution but fought against it. Notably amongst them were the Nonconformists. The first petition to Parliament against slavery was got up by a Cambridge Baptist minister.[14] Daniel Defoe denounced

[10] *Journal*, VI.211.
[11] *Letters*, VI.378.
[12] *Journal*, II.389.
[13] ibid., VI.123.
[14] See Carlile, *The Story of the English Baptists*, p. 172.

the slave trade in his *Reformation of Manners*, and urged the better treatment of negroes in his *Life of Colonel Jacque*. But the chief, most consistent, and most pertinacious of the opponents of slavery were the Quakers, who as early as 1671 were feeling out toward the idea of freeing the slaves.[15] In 1727, at their Yearly Meeting in London they ' censured ' the practice of Friends having anything to do with slave importation. Their attitude gradually hardens, until in 1761, and again in 1763, it was decided to exclude from the Society of Friends any who continued to be implicated in any way in the slave trade.[16] From the midst of the Friends came one of great importance in the history of Abolition, Anthony Benezet, originally a French Huguenot. His importance lay not only in his literary work against slavery, but in his influence upon Clarkson and Wesley in this regard.

Wesley had, however, been brought into contact with the question of slavery years before he read Benezet's works. In Georgia, his contact was close because although, as noted above, at that time slavery was not permitted in that colony, already there was agitation for its introduction. Some settlers were clamouring to be allowed to have slaves to work their plantations. These men are described by Curnock, the editor of John Wesley's *Journal* (Standard Edition), as ' unscrupulous ',[17] and no doubt some of them were quite without humanitarian or religious scruples; but the question which primarily concerned them was the economic. In other colonized parts of America, some of them near at hand, slave labour was the rule, and it appeared impossible for the colonists

---

[15] See George Fox, *Journal*, II.149 (1902, Bi-centenary edition).

[16] See Society of Friends, *Extracts from the Book of Christian Discipline of the Religious Society of Friends in Great Britain*, p. 159; and Barclay, *The Inner Life of the Religious Societies of the Commonwealth*, p. 554.

[17] op. cit., I.244n.

of Georgia to compete with those who had this cheap labour. The arguments that slave labour is really dear, because, being unwilling, it is bad, while the total costs of a slave are considerable, have great weight; but it was a long while before the truth in these arguments became apparent. Meanwhile, Oglethorpe, the Governor of Georgia, and Wesley together stood firmly by the Georgia Trustees in their prohibition of slavery in the colony. The Trustees were, however, unable to prevent 'a system of apprenticeship, or voluntary self-sale, or self-hiring for a term of years; and this led to abuses only less frightful than those which prevailed on the plantations of Carolina and Florida, where negro slaves worked'.[18] During his visits to South Carolina, Wesley saw coloured slavery at first hand. As may be expected, he was much concerned about the religious state of the slaves and questioned a number, male and female, finding most of them extremely ignorant as to the teaching of Christianity, even where, as in some cases, the slaves had been taken or sent regularly to Church. (It was, of course, one of the chief arguments of the apologists for slavery that it was for the good of the soul of the Black to be put as a slave to a Christian White. Wesley was able to see for himself how this worked out in practice.) Characteristically, he at once thinks out a scheme for the methodical handling of the situation. He advocates that inquiry should be made and the 'most serious' of the planters discovered. 'Then, having inquired of them which of their slaves were best inclined and understood English, to go to them from plantation to plantation, staying as long as appeared necessary at each. Three or four gentlemen at Carolina I have been with that would be sincerely glad of such an assistant, who might pursue his

[18] *Journal*, I.181n.

CONCERN WITH CERTAIN SOCIAL QUESTIONS

work with no more hindrances than must everywhere attend the preaching of the gospel.'[19]

Wesley's interest in the negroes remained, and indeed, grew. Occasional references to this interest appear, as when he preached in London (on the 29th June 1740 on Titus 3[8]) and had a collection for a negro school. He transcribes into his *Journal* a considerable part of a letter from the Rev. Samuel Davies, of Hanover, Virginia, with the comment: ' I was much affected about this time by a letter sent from a gentleman in Virginia.'[20] Mr. Davies commented sadly upon the fact that not only did the negro slaves arrive in America with no knowledge of the Christian religion, but most of their masters did not trouble about them in that respect. In particular, the writer noted that the masters would not go to the expense of getting suitable books for such as could read. Apparently Wesley, in response to this state of affairs, sent books, for another letter from Mr. Davies, some eight months later, describes the receipt and distribution of these books. ' All the books were very acceptable, but none more so than the *Psalms* and *Hymns*.' Davies notes that some of the masters, as a result of this interest from England in the welfare of their slaves, have now begun to get books for them.[21] Early in 1758, Wesley preached in the house of a Mr. Gilbert at Wandsworth, and notes with appreciation the apparent effect on Gilbert's two negro servants, and a mulatto. Some months later, when again at Wandsworth, he baptizes the negroes, with the comment: ' Shall not our Lord, in due time, have these heathens also " for His inheritance ".'[22] He notes with

[19] *Journal*, I.353.
[20] See ibid., IV.125-6.
[21] ibid., pp. 149-50.
[22] ibid., pp. 247, 292.

F

evident joy the presence in Society at Whitehaven, in 1780, of a negress. At Kingswood, in 1786, he baptizes another young negro.[23]

By pulpit, pamphlet, and letter, Wesley took a part in helping the anti-slavery cause. He wrote to the editor of the *Monthly Review*, in 1774, against the bad treatment meted out by the American owners to their slaves, and the same year saw the appearance of his *Thoughts upon Slavery*, some twelve years prior to the foundation of the ' Society for the Suppression of the Slave Trade '. In this important pamphlet, Wesley traces the history and geography of slavery, deals with the transportation of slaves and the legal position. In particular, he writes against the economic argument, noted above, of the necessity of slaves, especially urging that it is untrue to state that slaves are necessary in hot countries because the Whites cannot work there. He says that white men are quite capable of becoming inured to work in hot climates, by degrees, provided they are temperate in food and drink.[24] On 4th March 1788, in Bristol, so much of the fortune of which was built upon the slave trade, Wesley makes an announcement that he will preach two days later upon Slavery, which he notes ' is now the general topic '. When Thursday came, the building was packed. Half way through the sermon there was a strange experience, ' a vehement noise arose, none could tell why, and shot like lightning through the whole congregation. The terror and confusion were inexpressible. You might have imagined it was a city taken by storm. The people rushed upon each other with the utmost violence; the benches were broke in pieces, and nine-tenths of the

[23] ibid., VII.144.

[24] See Wesley, *Works*, XI.56-9; *Letters*, VI.126; and Bebb, op. cit., p. 160.

congregation appeared to be struck with the same panic. In about six minutes the storm ceased, almost as suddenly as it rose, and, all being calm, I went on'. His comment is that such an unprecedented incident could only be due to preternatural influence and was a sign that Satan was fighting 'lest his kingdom should be delivered up'. Whether as a result of this manifestation, or because it had been previously determined, the following day was observed as a day of fasting and prayer on behalf of the Black slaves, that their freedom might be given them.[25]

In August 1787 Wesley wrote to the Abolition Committee to inform them of his great satisfaction on hearing of their formation. He warned them to expect great opposition in their work and promised his help, to which end he would reprint a new large edition of his *Thoughts upon Slavery* and circulate it with a commendation of the objects of the Abolition Committee.[26] He followed this by a second letter, in October of the same year, in which he points out a weakness in the methods of the Abolition Society: 'And you may be assured these men will lay hold on and improve every possible objection against you. I have been afraid lest they (i.e. those engaged in the Slave Trade) should raise an objection from your manner of procuring information. To *hire* or to *pay* informers has a bad sound and might raise great, yea insurmountable, prejudice against you. Is it not worth your consideration whether it would not be advisable to drop this mode entirely, and to be content with such information as you can procure by more honourable means?' He also raises, in this letter, the point that the number of sailors who perish in the course of the trade should be considered as

[25] See *Journal*, VII.359–60.
[26] *Letters*, VIII.6–7.

an argument.[27] The following month we find he has followed up his letters to the Abolition Committee, for in a letter to one of his preachers, Thomas Funnell, he says: ' Whatever assistance I can give those generous men who join to oppose that execrable trade I certainly shall give. I have printed a large edition of the *Thoughts on Slavery*, and dispersed them to every part of England. But there will be vehement opposition made, both by slave-merchants and slave-holders; and they are mighty men. But our comfort is, He that dwelleth on high is mightier.'[28] He apparently succeeds in stimulating some of his followers to do their part, for early in 1790 he writes to Henry Moore (later to be one of Wesley's literary executors and biographers): ' I have received the parcel by the coach (? parcel of *Thoughts upon Slavery*). I quite approve of your sending the note to all our Assistants, and hope it will have a good effect. I would do anything that is in my power toward the extirpation of that trade which is a scandal not only to Christianity but humanity.'[29]

The last book Wesley read was *The Interesting Narrative of the Life of Olaudah Equiano, or Gustavus Vassa*, in two volumes. Wesley was one of the subscribers to this work, and he was reading it on his journey to Leatherhead, where he preached for the last time. It probably led him to write his often-quoted last letter, which was to Wilberforce, on this same subject, for in that letter he refers to the statement in this book he had been reading that in the West Indian courts a Black man's testimony against a White is not admissible as evidence. He urged Wilberforce

[27] ibid., p. 17.

[28] ibid., p. 23.

[29] ibid., p. 207. For a transcript of Wesley's will naming Moore as literary executor, together with Thomas Coke, and John Whitehead, see *Journal*, VIII.342-4.

to go on unrestingly with his work for negro emancipation.[30]

Wesley's sympathy for the slave, and detestation of the whole institution of slavery, had a good deal of effect, apart from the assistance to the Abolition cause which necessarily accrued from the adherence to it of so influential a man as he had become in his later years. Methodists, as was to be expected, followed the lead of their founder. Many actually gave up the use of sugar because it was ' a drug composed of the *slave-dealer's sin* and the *slave's misery* '.[31] Then in the year of Wesley's death, the Wesleyan Conference obtained 229,426 signatures to an anti-slavery petition, while those obtained by all other nonconformists, including the Roman Catholics, were only 122,978.[32] But there is another important point. During the years when the agitation against slavery was growing the number of Methodist missionaries and adherents on the other side of the Atlantic was growing as well as on this side. Many of these lived and worked in areas where there were many slaves, and moreover many of the slaves themselves were Methodists. Wesley's sympathy with the slaves might have been supposed to lead to indiscipline and disturbance amongst them, but apparently it tended to work the other way, for advertisements were sometimes found in the American papers offering for sale a slave and adding that he was a Methodist. It was not Wesley's way to make agitators, but rather to fight for those whose condition needed improvement, while encouraging them meanwhile to

---

[30] *Journal*, VIII.128.

[31] Thomas W. Blanshard, *Life of Samuel Bradburn: The Methodist Demosthenes*, p. 140.

[32] Quoted from *Wesley Studies*, p. 190 (by Maldwyn Edwards, *John Wesley and the Eighteenth Century*, p. 124).

remain, if not content, at least quiet and industrious. His attitude would be, not that any man had received a vocation from God to be a slave, but that if he were a slave, and so long as he remained such, he should regard his life vocationally, and accordingly work to the glory of God. And in doing so, he might be sure that Wesley, with his accustomed energy and fearlessness would be working for him. In fact, Methodists in America were already, before the death of Wesley, acting up to his convictions in this matter of slavery. Wesley is able to write to Samuel Hoare, in 1787, that: ' A week or two ago I was favoured with a letter from Mr. Clarkson, informing me of his truly Christian design, to procure, if possible, an Act of Parliament for the abolition of slavery in our Plantations. I have long wished for the rolling away of this reproach. . . . Especially when I read Mr. Benezet's tracts, and what Mr. Sharp has written upon the subject. My friends in America are of the same mind. They have already emancipated several hundred of the poor negroes, and are setting more and more at liberty every day, as fast as they can do it with any tolerable convenience. . . .'[33]

Wesley's attitude toward servants having bad masters was similar to his attitude toward slaves and masters—he approved neither of slave-owners nor of bad masters of any sort, but urged that servant and slave alike should, if they were Christians, serve the bad master with an eye to pleasing God. However different this attitude may be from that more prevalent to-day, it was quite consistent, and is quite understandable. Whether slavery, or anything else was the evil, Wesley's attitude was that matters would only be made worse by agitation. God could be, and must be, served in whatever condition of

[33] *Letters*, VIII.275.

PRISONS

During his Oxford days, John Wesley's father had visited the prisoners, and John himself began to do so a few months after he had returned to Oxford from his period at Epworth and Wroot, where he had acted as his father's curate. It was on the initiative of Morgan, his fellow-member of the 'Holy Club,' that, in 1730, Wesley began this work of prison visitation. Morgan had some time before begun various forms of philanthropic work in Oxford. Wesley records the beginnings of his activities in this direction, and also his hesitations about it. He wrote: 'On the 24th August 1730 my brother and I walked with him (i.e. Morgan) to the Castle. We were so well satisfied with our conversation there, that we agreed to go thither once or twice a week; which we had not done long, before he desired me to go with him to see a poor woman in the town who was sick. In this employment too, when we came to reflect upon it, we believed it would be worth while to spend an hour or two in a week.'[34] This marks the beginning of all his philanthropic and evangelistic work. He was doubtful of the propriety of what he was doing, even when it was done with the consent of the 'minister of the parish', and so he wrote for his father's advice. Samuel Wesley, senior, replied with warm commendation, adding the advice that the approval of Dr. Potter, the Bishop of Oxford, should be obtained, and this John got without difficulty. From that

[34] *Journal*, I.90.

time this work goes on steadily, also including the visitation of debtor prisoners in Bocardo, a jail which consisted of a room over the north gate of the city.[35]

John Gambold, who afterwards entered Holy Orders, and was up at Christ Church with Wesley, wrote later a description of the methods adopted by members of the Holy Club in their visitation of the prisoners. He says that one or other of them went to the Castle every day, and most days to Bocardo. He goes on: ' Whoever came to the Castle was to read in the chapel to as many prisoners as would attend, and to talk apart to the man or men whom he had taken particularly in charge. Before reading he asked, Whether they had prayers yesterday ? (For some serious man among the prisoners read family prayers with the rest.) Whether they had read over again what was read last, and what they remembered of it ? Then he went over the heads of it to them, and afterwards went on in the same book for a quarter of an hour (the books they used were the *Christian Monitor*, the *Country Parson's Advice to his Parishioners*, and such like);[36] and when he had done, he summed up the several particulars that had been insisted on, enforced the advice given, and reduced it at last to two or three sentences which they might easily remember. Then he took his man aside, and asked him, Whether he was in the chapel yesterday ? and other questions concerning his care to serve God, and learn his duty. . . . In order to release those who were confined for small debts, and were bettered by their affliction (and likewise to purchase books, physic, and other necessaries), they raised a little fund, to which

[35] See ibid., II.102.

[36] This parenthesis is Gambold's own. *The Christian Monitor containing an earnest exhortation to a holy life, with some directions in order thereunto*, by John Rawlet(t), was published in London in 1688. *The Country Parson's Advice* was published (in two parts) in 1680.

many of their acquaintance contributed quarterly.'[37] This is very interesting because although it is written of the activities of the group known as the Holy Club, the details set out by Gambold show unmistakably the impress of John Wesley. There can be no doubt that it was he who chiefly determined this scheme: it is so completely characteristic with its system, its care to press home what had been read and said, and its care for men one by one. In 1732, when Wesley was at Epworth with his father, John Clayton, another member of the Holy Club, writes to him a long letter, followed by another a month later, of which large parts are taken up with detailed information as to the progress of various named prisoners, progress spiritually, and in regard to the circumstances of their imprisonment.[38] After his return from Georgia, Wesley visits Oxford and immediately makes inquiries about the Castle and Bocardo and laments there is now no one to look after ' my poor prisoners '.

The duty of visiting prisoners was continually enforced by Wesley, not only by his example, but by urging the imperative character of New Testament injunctions, such as that implied in the passage of Matthew 25[31-46]. He records in his Diary how he visited persons in places as far apart as London, Bristol, Exeter, York, Carrickfergus, and Whitley.[39] To meet some of the spiritual needs of

---

[37] *Journal*, VIII.266–7 (Appendix 5).

[38] ibid., pp. 275–81 (Appendix 9), e.g. ' I got Mrs. Topping a copy of her son's indictment at the assizes, which has made her mighty easy ever since. . . . Tempro is discharged, and I have appointed Harris to read to the prisoners in his stead. Two of the felons likewise have paid their fees, and are gone out, both of them able to read mighty well. There are only two in the jail who want this accomplishment . . . I hear them both read (i.e. their letters) three times a week ' (loc. cit., pp. 276–7).

[39] Many of them he visited on numerous occasions.

prisoners, special hymns were written and published.[40] In this work of prison visitation, it may be noted, Charles Wesley was particularly active and successful.

Primarily, it is true, Wesley, and the Methodists generally after him, were concerned with the souls of prisoners, and this is particularly shown by their activities with the condemned felons, whom they would sometimes accompany to the scaffold. When, as not infrequently happened, these men, and women too, were brought to a condition of repentance and faith in their last few hours of life, particular satisfaction would be registered. Nevertheless, it would be a serious misreading of the situation to imagine that this concern was of a purely religious character. Wesley was interested in men as men, as well as men as souls; indeed, had it not been so, it is incredible that he would have held the tremendous interest and devotion of people. The soul was the centre, but not the circumference of his interest, and the range of subjects covered by his manifold publications is evidence of this, especially those having to do with medicine. His *Primitive Physic*, first published in 1747, with its emphasis on the value of exercise as a means of maintaining health, on cold-water baths as a cure for numerous diseases, and his experimental interest in the curative possibilities of electricity, is incompatible with the idea that he was only concerned with souls, and from the first his evangelistic and pastoral work amongst prisoners was accompanied by what we should now call medical services.

We must now notice some instances of early Methodist workers in prisons, of whom by far the most important is Dagge, the jailer of Newgate, Bristol. This man became a Methodist in the first instance under the preaching of

[40] *Hymns of Intercession for all Mankind* (1758), No. 27; *Hymns and Sacred Poems*, by Charles Wesley (1749), Vol. I, No. 100.

Whitefield. But Wesley used to visit him periodically, and the prisoners in his charge, and noted with great approval the change which had come over the prison since 1737 when Dagge, its keeper, had been converted. In twenty years its whole character had been altered. Wesley made a careful inspection of it in October 1760, prefacing his description of its condition with an exclamation at the difference since he first knew it.[41] He states that now it had become ' as clean and sweet as a gentleman's house ' for every prisoner had twice a week to cleanse thoroughly his ' apartment'. In many jails there were fighting and brawling, but not so here, because whenever differences occurred between prisoners they were immediately referred to Dagge, who settled the matter on the spot, after hearing both sides. Besides, the usual causes of prisoners' quarrels, cheating and other ' wrongs ', had largely ceased since the rule was enforced that any such delinquencies, when discovered, resulted in the closer incarceration of the guilty party. Wesley further notes that no drunkenness was allowed, and adds significantly, ' however advantageous it might be to the keeper and tapster '—for in almost all prisons of the period drunkenness was actually encouraged because of the profit to those in authority there. Another improvement noted is that no immorality was permitted, the women prisoners being kept separate from the men, and no prostitute being admitted, ' no, not at any price '.

On the positive side, Wesley remarks that industry was encouraged by the provision of tools and materials on reasonable terms, and by the impartial division of the alms given by the charitable. He notes, too, that at that particular time, a shoemaker, tailor, brazier, and even a coach-maker were all working at their trades. No work

[41] *Journal*, IV.416.

was permitted on Sundays, attendance at Divine Service being compulsory, and a sermon was preached in addition every Thursday. In conclusion Wesley states: 'By the blessing of God on these regulations, the whole prison has a new face. Nothing offends either the eye, or ear, and the whole has the appearance of a quiet, serious family.'[42]

The importance of Dagge's work is considerable. It shows the way in which a man converted under Methodism found his religious experience leading him to regard his occupation as a vocation, and using the opportunities of his position for social reform. Dagge's concern for his soul, and the souls of those in his charge, was inseparably accompanied by a regimentation of life notable for restraint, cleanliness, and useful employment. But its importance does not stop there, for a comparison between what he was actually doing in the Bristol Newgate and the reforms advocated by that outstanding prison reformer, Howard, show a close correspondence. And these reforms urged by Howard were fifteen years later than the time when Dagge had already got his prison into the improved condition described above. Further, Howard was certainly acquainted with the Bristol Newgate.[43] It may be added that Wesley and Howard were in touch with one another, and that the former had a great admiration for the work of the latter. On one occasion, in 1787, Wesley records: 'I had the pleasure of a conversation with Mr. Howard, I think one of the greatest men in Europe. Nothing but the mighty power of God can enable him to

---

[42] ibid., p. 417; cf. also Simon: *The Revival of Religion in England in the Eighteenth Century* (1907), pp. 292–3; Samuel Johnson, *Lives of the English Poets—Life of Savage*, II.423–4, 429. See also Bebb, op. cit., pp. 153–4.

[43] See John Howard, *The State of the Prisons in England and Wales*, especially pp. 31, 32, 41, 43, 51.

go through his difficult and dangerous employments.'[44]

Methodists were frequently exhorted in sermons to visit and otherwise help prisoners. Many of them did, and some devoted much time over a period of years to this charitable enterprise. Notable amongst them was a woman, Sarah Peters, who died in the beginning of November 1748, rendering her services for prisoners, and particularly for those condemned to death, up to the last. She probably died of the 'jail distemper' caught from these visitations. She behaved in the way Wesley was constantly urging, the way of giving service to the body while greatly concerned with the soul, and showed this double concern clearly in the case of John Lancaster: 'Some being of opinion it would not be difficult to procure a pardon for him, S. Peters, though she never mentioned this to him, resolved to leave no means unattempted. She procured several petitions to be drawn, and went herself to Westminster, to Kensington, and to every part of the town where anyone lived who might possibly assist therein. In the meantime she went constantly to Newgate, sometimes alone, sometimes with one or two others, visited all that were condemned in their cells, exhorted them, prayed with them.'[45] Her efforts to save Lancaster from execution were not, in fact, successful.

One of those referred to as being taken by Sarah Peters to Newgate was Silas Told, who was for some time master of Wesley's school at the Foundery, London. Of him, Wesley writes: 'I buried what was mortal of honest Silas Told (this was in December 1778). For many years he attended the malefactors in Newgate, without fee or reward; and I suppose no man for this hundred years has been so successful in that melancholy office. God had

[44] *Journal*, VII.295.
[45] ibid., III.381-7.

given him peculiar talents for it; and he had amazing success therein. The greatest part of those whom he attended died in peace, and many of them in the triumph of faith.'[46]

EDUCATION

Wesley was essentially an educationist, in this sense, that his own mind was always seeking to assimilate new facts and to relate them to old knowledge, while he was always as keen to teach others as to learn himself. His logical bent and training and his skill as a systematizer ensured that what knowledge he had should be passed on in suitable form. The educational maxim, ' No impression without expression ', is one that he would have welcomed, for his own impressions not only were constantly being expressed, and being deepened in the process, but he taught his preachers themselves to be learners and teachers. His interest in education, and his service of its aims, were not in the least diminished as a result of that experience of his which is commonly called his ' evangelical conversion '. However personal and direct his appeals, and however much he might use emotion in them, and expect emotional responses, he did not cease to be fundamentally a teacher. Rather, he harnessed the emotional forces he evoked to educational uses. However little they might have realized it, his converts were committed to a rigorous form of adult education which should not cease while they had life. The converts were gathered into bands and classes, and these fellowships were not only means of maintaining and developing spiritual experience, and of teaching and enforcing

[46] ibid., VI.221. See also *An Account of the Life and Dealings of God with Silas Told. . . . written by Himself* (Salford 1806).

discipline—they were also important educational influences. Wesley's purpose in gathering men and women into these societies was not educational in intention—it was to save their souls and to lead them to forms of service appropriate to saved people—but its technique was an educational technique, and none the less so because it was something quite new to the vast majority of converts.

How quick he was to seize opportunities in this direction is illustrated by his action in London, in 1745: ' We had ', he wrote, ' within a short time given away some thousands of little tracts among the common people. And it pleased God hereby to provoke others to jealousy. In so much that the Lord Mayor (i.e. Sir Henry Marshal) had ordered a large quantity of papers, dissuading from cursing and swearing, to be printed and distributed to the train-bands (who were then quartered near Wesley's Chapel at the Foundery). And this day *An Earnest Exhortation to Serious Repentance* was given at every church door, in or near London, to every person who came out, and one left at the house of every householder who was absent from church.'[47] This occurred in connexion with the National Fast of the 18th December 1745, the Pretender having reached Derby. Under the circumstances, it did not require Wesley to stir people up to an unwonted degree of religious observance, but it was he who immediately saw the opportunity presented for an appeal by the written word to the public generally.

Wesley really believed in education. He believed in knowledge as opposed to ignorance and he believed in training people to think for themselves. He had considerable experience of the truth of the adage, ' A little learning is a dangerous thing ', for not infrequently one

[47] *Journal*, III.228.

or other of his preachers (for the most part men of very inferior educational background—although this was not true of them all), having obtained a little book-knowledge, would make a fool of himself and would have to be rebuked. But Wesley never despaired and steadily proceeded on the assumption that the cure of the evils springing from a little knowledge is more knowledge. Indeed, what he expected his preachers to study, and what he expected other people to read, as shown by the subject-matter of the volumes of the works he published, is amazing. He never committed the error of 'talking (or writing) down' to people. His sermons are models of concise thought and appeal based on reasons advanced, and are remarkable for the demands they make upon their hearers for concentrated thinking.[48] The title of one of his famous pamphlets—*An Appeal to Men of Reason and Religion* (and its sequel, *A Further Appeal* . . .)—is indicative of the way in which his mind worked.

Moreover, Wesley was a pioneer of popular education. As usual, his prime concern was with the soul, since he believed that intellectual knowledge and true religion were companions. But, also as usual, his concern and

[48] The question arises, however, as to whether Wesley's sermons were delivered in the form in which they now appear. This is very unlikely, for one reason, because Wesley sometimes quotes from original languages: (e.g. Sermon on 1 John 5^{20}, subject, 'God and Eternal Life': 'How little do we know of His methods of government? Only this we know, "Ita praesides singulis sicut universis, et universis sicut singulis!"' In this case he gives a translation, but in the same sermon he quotes "Magnam Mens agitans molem, et vasto se corpore miscens" with no translation (*Arminian Magazine* (1781), IV.132–3).) Such quotations, even when their translation is suggested to an educated person by the context, would be completely meaningless to a crowd of Kingswood miners or to most of the congregations to whom he preached. Further, there are extremely few illustrations in most of the printed sermons, whereas preaching to popular audiences, often in the street, almost demands the use of illustration on a somewhat extensive scale. On the other hand, all Wesley's writings and recorded conversations show his consistent appeal to hard thinking. Probably his printed sermons were revised editions of those spoken.

activities did not stop there, as the range of his publications makes clear. What is particularly remarkable is that his work for education was so complete, both horizontally as regards subjects taught, and vertically as regards the organization of instruction. The subjects spread out on all sides; the organization started from the illiterate at the bottom and went right up through the whole process of providing books. This provision of books involved writing, preparing, and publishing them, and then marketing them. Wesley did not normally aim at adult classes, but at adult readers; he did not aim at bringing people to books, but books to people. Many of the Methodist converts were illiterate, but few were allowed to remain content in that state. They were encouraged, and very successfully, to learn to read in order to be able to read the Bible. And they did read their Bibles—a liberal education in itself. Even in the case of those who remained illiterate, a real educational process was at work in them through the Scriptural language and ideas with which they were saturated in these weekly fellowships. Wesley himself was sometimes surprised at the result. Thus he notes, in 1782, at Kingswood, where he met the Bands after preaching at the School: 'The colliers spoke without any reserve. I was greatly surprised; not only the matter of what they spoke was rational and scriptural, but the language, yea, and the manner, were exactly proper. Who teacheth like Him?'[49] Three years later, in London, similarly he notes: 'We had a lovefeast. I could not but observe the manner wherein several of them spoke one after another. Not only the matter, but the language, the accent, the

[49] ibid., VI.344; cf. Acts 4[13]: 'When they beheld the boldness of Peter and John, and had perceived that they were unlearned and ignorant men, they marvelled; and they took knowledge of them, that they had been with Jesus' (R.V.).

tone of voice, wherewith illiterate persons, men and women, young and old, spoke, were such as a scholar need not be ashamed of.'[50]

Wesley wrote pamphlets and books on many subjects, or, no less often, abridged the works of others. Thus, he put on the market *A Short English Grammar* at the price of one penny, and also put out short Latin, French, Greek, and Hebrew grammars. These grammars of foreign languages were for use at his Kingswood School, for lower forms, and also for his preachers. In 1753, Wesley published a *Complete English Dictionary*, and twenty-three years later, a *Concise History of England* in four volumes. In some ways most remarkable of all was his *Primitive Physick*, already referred to, and which was first published in 1747, afterwards going through twenty-three editions in his lifetime. He employed his unique organization as a means of marketing books, insisting that his travelling preachers should carry constantly in their saddle-bags supplies of books for sale or, in some cases, for free distribution. Thus he anticipated the modern bookstall so often in evidence at religious and other conventions. Wesley's books found their way into the homes of thousands of people who otherwise would have read little or nothing.

In addition to this direct work of education for which he was responsible, Wesley was an indirect educator through his preachers. These men came from a variety of educational backgrounds. A few had had as good an education as could be obtained, but the majority were neither the products of the Universities, nor of the Dissenting Academies; they were in fact from an intellectual point of view much nearer those to whom they ministered. But they were all encouraged, or rather, were

[50] ibid., VII.49.

commanded, to spend several hours each day in real study, and they knew that they would have to answer to Wesley in this matter. He would no more tolerate ignorance in his preachers than he would condone idleness. He who impressed upon them that they had nothing to do except save souls, at the same time bade them study Hebrew and Greek; they were to be evangelists, not ignorant ranters. This has real importance because the sermon of those days, amongst Methodists at least, was a real training in mental discipline and thought processes. Wesley wrote in disgust and contempt of those who obtained a trifling popularity by preaching ' Gospel Sermons ', in which, he said, they talked in a meaningless fashion about the ' blood of Christ '. Instead of this type of thing, he never wearied in training his men to make the best use of their homiletical resources so that they might present religion in a reasoned way.

Important as is the presentation of the Gospel by Wesley and his preachers from a religious point of view, it is also of considerable importance from the standpoint of popular education, seeing that the sermons their followers so frequently heard provided one of the few opportunities for directed thinking and the relation of one activity of life to others. The Methodist pulpit and classroom gave simple men and women not only a theology but also something of a philosophy of living. Wesley, in an important letter,[51] deals at length with his understanding of what was involved in ' preaching the gospel '. This letter was written in 1751 (to whom is not known for certain—perhaps to Ebenezer Blackwell, his banker friend), and was a considered reply to a letter he had received some while before. In it, Wesley says: ' I mean by " preaching the gospel " preaching the love of God to

[51] *Letters*, III.79–85.

sinners, preaching the life, death, resurrection, and intercession of Christ, with all the blessings which in consequence thereof are freely given to true believers. . . . I think the right method of preaching is this. At our first beginning to preach at any place, after a general declaration of the love of God to sinners and His willingness that they should be saved, to preach the law in the strongest, the closest, the most searching manner possible; only intermixing the gospel here and there, and showing it, as it were, afar off. After more and more persons are convinced of sin, we may mix more and more of the gospel. . . . But when these grow in grace and in the knowledge of Christ, a wise builder would preach the law to them again. . . . Thus would he preach the law even to those who were pressing on to the mark. . . . Not that I would advise to preach the law without the gospel, any more than the gospel without the law. Undoubtedly both should be preached in their turns; yea, both at once, or both in one. All the conditional promises are instances of this. They are law and gospel mixed together. According to this model, I should advise every preacher continually to preach the law—the law grafted upon, tempered by, and animated with the spirit of the gospel. I advise him to declare, explain, and enforce every command of God. But meantime to declare in every sermon (and the more explicitly the better) that the first and great command to a Christian is, " Believe in the Lord Jesus Christ ": that Christ is all in all, our *wisdom, righteousness, sanctification, and redemption*; that all life, love, strength, are from Him alone, and all freely given to us through faith. . . . And upon this plan all the *Methodists* first set out.' Wesley then goes on to compare this method, with its demands upon the intelligence of the hearers, with the so-called ' gospel preachers ', who, he alleges, 'corrupt their hearers; they vitiate their taste, so that they cannot relish sound doctrine; and spoil their appetite, so that they cannot turn it into nourishment; ... they give them cordial upon cordial. ... Hence it is that (according to the constant observation I have made in all parts both of England and Ireland) preachers of this kind (though quite the contrary appears at first) spread death, not life, among their hearers. ... This was the very case when I went last into the North. For some time before my coming John Downes[52] had scarce been able to preach at *all*: the three others in the Round were such as styled themselves " gospel preachers ". When I came to review the Societies, with great expectation of finding a vast increase, I found most of them lessened by one third. ... Such were the blessed effects of this *gospel-preaching*, of this *new* method of *preaching Christ*. On the other hand, when in my return I took an account of the Societies in Yorkshire, chiefly under the care of John Nelson, one of the *old* way, in whose preaching you could find no life, no food, I found them all alive, strong, and vigorous of soul, believing, loving, and praising God their Saviour, and increased in number from eighteen or nineteen hundred to upwards of three thousand. ... This is the scriptural way, the *Methodist* way, the true way. ... '

This letter shows the way in which Wesley would have his preachers do their work. They were not to present the Gospel in such a soothing way as made no demands upon either the thought or conduct of the auditors. On the contrary, it was to be proclaimed as a message from God which demanded a total response, of mind, heart, and

---

[52] John Downes was one of the preachers who had been affected by James Wheatley, a man whose character as well as whose preaching gave great offence (see *Journal*, III.531-3; IV.96).

will. So presented it could not fail to be an educative force of considerable value.

Wesley's education of his preachers was not confined to the provision of books and the insistence that they should be studied, and to advice and discipline in respect of their preaching; he also occasionally organized short Courses for them. One of these was held as early as Lent 1749, at the school at Kingswood. ' My design ', he says, ' was to have as many of our preachers here during the Lent as could possibly be spared; and to read lectures to them every day, as I did to my pupils in Oxford. I had seventeen of them in all. These I divided into two classes, and read to one Bishop Pearson on *The Creed*, to the other Aldrich's *Logic*, and to both *Rules for Action and Utterance*.'[53] Charles Wesley, in a letter written at that time, refers to this enterprise: ' I spent half an hour with my brother at Kingswood, which is now very much like a college. Twenty-one boarders are there and a dozen students, his sons and pupils in the gospel. I believe he is now laying the foundations of many generations.'[54] The discrepancy between Charles Wesley's figure of twelve and his brother's of seventeen students, is most probably due to the former, who was only there half an hour, making a rough estimate of the round figure of a dozen, instead of actually counting heads.

Much of the verbal, or class instruction, of Wesley's preachers had to proceed with the minimum of prearrangement, Wesley seizing opportunities as they occurred. Glimpses of this appear every now and then. In November 1756, for instance, we find he ' began reading over, with the preachers that were in town, Mr. Pike's *Philosophia Sacra* ', while the next month he

[53] *Journal*, III.391.
[54] Tyerman, *Life and Times of John Wesley*, II.34n.

'read with the preachers this week the Glasgow Abridgement of Mr. Hutchinson's *Works*', and in January 1757 he reads to them 'the late Bishop of Cork's excellent *Treatise on Human Understanding*' (the Bishop was Dr. Peter Browne, who held that See 1710–35). As the editor of the *Standard Journal* remarks, Wesley 'made the itinerancy a peripatectic school of learning'.[55] But Wesley did more than that. He not only made it possible for his preachers from time to time to have these short courses, but through them, as well as in other ways, including disciplinary action, he taught these men how to study when alone, and infused many with a real desire to gain knowledge, and to impart it to others. The value of this may be reflected in Wesley's observation, quoted above, of the way in which uneducated, or even illiterate, converts, could express themselves in open meetings. He educated people directly through his books and indirectly through his preachers, determined, in one way or another, to have a following whose mental powers should be so developed that they would not be shaken by every wind of doctrine which might happen to blow. In aiming at this, too, he did much to inspire people with some desire for knowledge apart from its direct connexion with religious teaching.

Great as may have been his success as a popular adult educator, the same cannot be said of his work as an educator of children. He began in a very small way to instruct children at Oxford, but it was not until he was in Germany in 1738 that he saw something that determined him upon setting up schools as an adjunct to other work. In July of that year he went to Halle, and going over Francke's Orphan House noted with great approval the building which reached 'backward from the front

[55] *Journal*, IV.190–2.

in two wings for, I believe, a hundred and fifty yards. The lodging-chambers for the children, their dining-room, their chapel, and all the adjoining apartments, are so conveniently contrived, and so exactly clean, as I have never seen any before. Six hundred and fifty children, we were informed, are wholly maintained there; and three thousand, if I mistake not, taught. Surely, such a thing neither we nor our fathers have known as this great thing which God has done here!'[56] He notes in his *Journal* the plan of education adopted in these Christian German schools,[57] in which more time was given to religious instruction than to any other subject. Ten months later, in the summer of 1739, he made a beginning of child educational work. It was only in that March that Wesley had received a call to go to Bristol and help in the evangelistic work being done there by Whitefield. He was reluctant to go, but he went, and it is significant that within three months he began to build a school—for the children of the Kingswood colliers. It became necessary to enlarge the school before many years had passed, and in June 1748 the opening ceremony of the new buildings was held at which Wesley preached on 'train up a child in the way he should go; and when he is old, he will not depart from it'.[58] No text could have been more appropriate because it expressed the basic educational maxim which governed all Wesley's schemes for school work. When these services were over, he and his brother Charles got together and drew up the general rules of the school.[59]

The background and object of these Rules appears in

[56] ibid., II.17.
[57] ibid., pp. 60–1.
[58] Proverbs 22[6].
[59] *Journal*, III.356.

CONCERN WITH CERTAIN SOCIAL QUESTIONS

an account of Kingswood School which John Wesley wrote much later for the *Arminian Magazine*.[60] In that article he states that he was led by the reading of one or two tracts on education, to consider the methods adopted in the schools of highest repute in the land. He notes, disapprovingly, that most of them were in centres of population, thus supplying too many distractions for the scholars; that children were admitted even when their parents had no real religious interest, a state of things paralleled, he says, by the irreligion of many of the masters. He then goes on to assert that it is not only in matters of religion, but also in learning, that these distinguished schools were deficient: ' In some, the children are taught little or no *Arithmetic*; in others, little care is taken even of their *Writing*. In many, they learn scarce the Elements of *Geography*, and as little of *Chronology*. And even as to the Languages, there are some schools of note, wherein no *Hebrew* at all is taught. . . . The Books which they read are not well chosen. . . . '[61]

Finding no school without these blemishes, he says, he determined to set up a school himself, one which should combine a definitely religious atmosphere and purpose with the most thorough teaching. Nothing could be more characteristic than Wesley's method with regard to admission of pupils: ' I next considered, How to procure proper *Scholars*: not any that came to hand, but, if possible, such as had some thoughts of God, and some desire of saving their souls: and such whose Parents desired they should not be almost, but altogether Christians. This was proposed to them, before their Children came: and to prevent future misunderstandings, they were desired attentively to read, and seriously to

[60] *Arminian Magazine*, Vol. IV (1781), pp. 381–4, 432–5, 486–93.
[61] ibid., pp. 383–4.

consider the Rules of the School; being assured they would be punctually observed, without any favour or affection. One of these rules was, that "no child shall be admitted after he is twelve years old". The ground of this rule was, A child could not well before that age be rooted either in bad habits, or ill principles. But notwithstanding the strictness of the Rules, I had soon as many Scholars as I desired. . . . ' Once accepted, a child was not removed even for a day until the parents removed him permanently.[62]

The Rules prescribed that all the children should rise at 4 a.m., summer and winter. 'They spend the time till five in private; partly in reading, partly in singing, partly in prayer: and in self-examination and meditation, those that are capable of it.' Then, at 5 o'clock they were brought all together, the next two hours passing in work, breakfasting, and walking. 'As we have no play-days, the School being taught every day in the year but Sundays, so neither do we allow any time for play on any day. . . . The school hours are from seven to eleven, and from one to five. . . . At eight they go to bed, the youngest first. They all lodge in one room (every Child having a bed to himself), in which a lamp burns all night. A master lies in the same room. . . . All their beds have mattresses on them, not feather-beds: both because they are more healthy, and because we would keep them at the utmost distance from softness and effeminacy.' In addition to the above allocation of daily time, when fine the scholars worked in the garden, and when wet, they did household tasks.[63]

The subjects taught comprised reading, writing, arithmetic; English, French, Latin, Greek, Hebrew;

[62] ibid. (1781), IV.433-4.
[63] ibid., pp. 434-5.

history, geography, chronology; rhetoric, logic, ethics; geometry, algebra, natural philosophy, and metaphysics. Wesley states that ever since he read Milton's ' admirable treatise on education ', he had been convinced that every youth ought to begin and finish his education at the same place, but he adds: ' I had so strong a prejudice in favour of our own universities, that of *Oxford* in particular, that I could hardly think of anyone's finishing his education, without spending some years there. I therefore encouraged all I had any influence over, to enter at *Oxford* or *Cambridge*.'[64]

Wesley was soon to discover that running a school, especially from a distance, with visits at irregular intervals, gave rise to all manner of difficulties, both with the staff and the scholars, but nothing was allowed to deter him. ' From the very beginning I met with all sorts of discouragements. . . . Notwithstanding which, through God's help, I went on; wrote an English, a Latin, a Greek, a Hebrew, and a French Grammar, and printed *Praelectiones Pueriles*, with many other books for the use of the School; and God gave a manifest blessing. Some of the wildest children were struck with deep conviction; all appeared to have good desires; and two or three began to taste the love of God.'[65] But many did not, and Wesley was driven from time to time to expel children from the school just as he would expel unsatisfactory adults from the Societies. One such child, expelled in 1750, he describes as ' exquisitely wicked '.

Wesley shared the general view of his day that a child was a small edition of an adult, but his attitude toward child education, in so far as it derived from others as distinct from his own observation and adaptation, was due

[64] ibid., pp. 487–8.
[65] *Journal*, III.530.

to his mother's influence. He had a lively recollection of both the moral and educational training received at home, and as early as 1732 wrote to Susanna Wesley asking for the details of her plan, and this she sent to him at considerable length. In this document Mrs. Wesley lays down her fundamental principle that 'in order to form the minds of children, the first thing to be done is to conquer their will, and bring them to an obedient temper. To inform the understanding is a work of time . . . but the subjecting the will is a thing that must be done at once, and the sooner the better. . . . I insist upon conquering the will of children betimes, because this is the only strong and rational foundation of a religious education, without which both precept and example will be ineffectual. But when this is thoroughly done, then a child is capable of being governed by the reason and piety of its parents, till its own understanding comes to maturity, and the principles of religion have taken root in the mind. . . . As self-will is the root of all sin and misery, so whatever cherishes this in children ensures their after-wretchedness and irreligion. . . . Heaven or hell depends on this alone. So that the parent who studies to subdue it in his child works together with God in the renewing and saving a soul.'[66] This important extract shows the principle on which Wesley himself based his schools. But it should be noted that neither the aim nor the effect of this method was to crush the personality; it was to crush self-will and selfishness in order—putting it in modern terms—that the personality might be developed. In fact this happened with the Wesleys, most of whom grew up to be, in a greater or less degree, determined, self-reliant, and even assertive. It was the same with the discipline exercised by Wesley over adult members of his Societies; his object

[66] ibid., III.35–6.

was certainly not to fit in a strait-jacket, but to develop; and in the main this object was notably attained.

Whatever case may be made out for this ' breaking of the will ' of children, none can be advanced for the way in which a child's religious experience was expected to approximate to that of an adult—and in Wesley's schools, religious experience was a most important part of the educational training. He records with great approval the words of a little boy who said: ' Mamma, I shall go to heaven soon, and be with the little angels.'[67] His own practice might be expected to lead to a similar type of thing, for when in Bristol, he was wont to set apart an hour weekly for meeting the children of his four schools there together. ' We soon found the effect of it in the children, some of whom were deeply and lastingly affected.'[68] But he also gave a good deal of time to educational work for them. In addition to the books mentioned above, some of which were prepared in the first instance for the Kingswood schools, here is a record of ten days spent there. He selected passages of Milton for the eldest children to learn; similarly, passages from *Moral and Sacred Poems*; he marks what he considers worth reading in the school from Dr. Basil Kennet(t)'s *Antiquities of Rome*; he revises for children's use Archbishop Potter's[69] *Grecian Antiquities* and also Thomas Lewis's *Hebrew Antiquities*; then he abridges Dr. William Cave's *Primitive Christianity*, probably for both adult and

---

[67] *Journal*, III.244.

[68] ibid., p. 392; cf. V.340-1: ' I inquired into the state of Kingswood School. The grievance now is the number of children. Instead of thirty (as I desired), we have near fifty; whereby our masters are burdened. And it is scarce possible to keep them in so exact order as we might do a smaller number. However, this still comes nearer a Christian school than any I know in the kingdom '.

[69] Formerly Bishop of Oxford (see pp. 6 and 80 *supra*).

school use; and he prepares a short *History of England* and a short *Roman History*.[70]

POVERTY AND CHARITY

In Wesley's life-time a change is observable in the general attitude toward the poor. At the beginning of the eighteenth century they were commonly regarded as belonging to one or other of three classes: those poor through injury or sickness; the aged; and the able-bodied. The third of these classes was the one which occasioned most controversy, as one might expect, and the usual view came to be that generally speaking the able-bodied unemployed were a nuisance, that is, that it was their own fault they were unemployed. But by the end of the period a more sympathetic attitude was common because the expansion of trade which at the beginning of the century and for some time after meant that the demand for workmen was keen, gave way to a more confused economic situation, as the Industrial Revolution began to make its progress more and more perceptible. Consequently there was a strong tendency to regard the poor as unfortunate rather than lazy.

Many were the schemes advocated, and sometimes forwarded, by religious people for the relief and the employment of the poor,[71] and it is not strange to find that Wesley, as will be noted, also tried both by his pen and by practical schemes to promote industry and employment and to relieve necessity. His chief importance, however, in this connexion lies in his attitude toward rich

---

[70] See ibid., 496, 499.

[71] Notable amongst such advocates were Thomas Firmin (1632–97) and John Bellers (1655?–1725)—see *Some Proposals for the Employing of the Poor*, by the former, and *Proposals for Raising a College of Industry*, and numerous other works, by the latter. Firmin was a Unitarian and Bellers a Quaker.

and poor respectively, and his association, almost identification, with the poor. He was a leader of the poor, especially the thrifty poor, greater than any other in the century.

The comparative poverty of his own upbringing, at times involving an actual shortage of food, or at least a threat of it; the period when as an undergraduate at Oxford he never had much money, and often too little; the experiences in Georgia, when at one time he was reduced to his last shilling[72]—all these had their effect on his attitude toward the poor and, no less important, on his ability to enter into their actual circumstances and fears. Many a man, after these experiences, would later have taken the opportunities which Wesley had of securing himself, as he legitimately could have done, at least a certain competency. This he did not do, although he secured the financial position of his brother Charles on the marriage of the latter. Indeed, he appeared to have almost a morbid desire to die leaving no estate behind him, and in fact what he had to dispose of under his will was extremely little. The truth is that, like his father, John Wesley often knew the need of money, but possessed a complete confidence that he would manage, somehow or other, come what may. This confidence was undoubtedly based in both cases, father and son, upon a firm belief in Providence, a belief to which they would give utterance from time to time. Poverty they knew, and Providence they knew, and they neither feared the former nor doubted the latter. Perhaps the sanguine temperament, possessed by these two Wesleys, might have accounted in part for this outlook. Yet John Wesley

[72] He writes in Georgia, 1st November 1737: 'Colonel Stephens arrived, by whom I received a benefaction of £10 sterling; after having been for several months without one shilling in the house, but not without peace, health, and contentment' (*Journal*, I.398).

had a fear in regard to money matters. He had no doubt that the grace of Christ was sufficient for the salvation of a rich man, but a reader of his *Journal* may be pardoned for thinking that Wesley regarded such a task as being only just within the compass of the divine grace. So he kept most careful account of all his receipts and expenditure, a practice not abandoned until 1790, when he stated that having kept his accounts for eighty-six years he was now 'satisfied with the continual conviction that I save all I can, and give all I can, that is, all I have'. It has been pointed out by a recent writer that as Wesley was eighty-seven years of age in 1790, his statement would mean that he began to keep accounts of 'his infant pence' at the age of one year. Allowing for the obvious exaggeration, it would seem that Mrs. Susanna Wesley trained her children from the earliest possible age to a serious stewardship of money.[73]

We must now note more particularly Wesley's attitude toward wealth (in however relative a degree possessed) and the rich. He was, in his earlier days, afraid of what its effects might be on himself. He comments upon his arrival at Charlestown, on his way home from America to England, where he had expected opposition and poor entertainment, if indeed any, but found what he considered 'far more dangerous; contempt and hunger being easy to be borne: but who can bear respect and fullness of bread?'[74] Returned to England he talks to a lady who was 'so much of a gentlewoman that for near an hour our labour seemed to be in vain'; however, after that the lady was 'moved'.[75] In May 1739, preaching at Clifton, Bristol, Wesley observed many rich

[73] ibid., VIII.80, 85; G. Elsie Harrison, *Son to Susanna*, p. 320.
[74] ibid., I.412.
[75] ibid., p. 446.

CONCERN WITH CERTAIN SOCIAL QUESTIONS

present, and felt troubled, ' earnestly desirous that some even of them ' might be saved.[76] The month following, after an encounter with Beau Nash, at Bath, he was informed that a number of wealthy ladies wished to speak to him. ' I went to them and said: " I believe, ladies, the maid mistook; you only wanted to look at me. ... I do not expect that the rich and great should want either to speak with me or to hear me; for I speak the plain truth—a thing you hear little of, and do not desire to hear." '[77] At Blackheath, the same month, he is ' moved with compassion for the rich ' who were present, observing that while some listened others ' drove away (in) their coaches from so uncouth a preacher '.[78] At Newcastle, he observed, with a mixture of gladness and irony, that God is doing something new in the world, for even some of the rich are being converted.[79] At Astbury, he comments approvingly on the manners of the ' many fine people ' in his congregation, who behaved ' as seriously as the poor ploughmen '.[80] He frequently draws this contrast between the manners of the rich and the poor, and at Clara, in Ireland, just as at Astbury, he notices with something akin to surprise the good behaviour of those listeners who had arrived in coaches.[81] At Athlone, however, he notes that only one person in the congregation kept his hat on, ' a gentleman of £700 or £800 a year '.[82] Back in London, at the Foundery chapel, at a watch-night service many of the rich were there, drawing from Wesley the question: ' Who hath warned you to

[76] ibid., II.201.
[77] ibid., p. 213.
[78] ibid., pp. 220-1.
[79] ibid., III.289-90.
[80] ibid., pp. 296, 299.
[81] ibid., p. 340.
[82] ibid., p. 343.

flee from the wrath to come?'[83] His suspicion of the motives and character of the rich was balanced by his contempt for their intelligence. At Anglesey, for an evening service: 'I was surprised to see, instead of some poor, plain people, a room full of men daubed with gold and silver. That I might not go out of their depth, I began expounding the story of Dives and Lazarus.' After the service, he adds that he spent a comfortable hour with some 'plain, honest Welshmen'.[84] Preaching near Dublin, he had the Earl of Drogheda and others of the gentry in the congregation who listened for a while, 'but it was not to their taste'.[85]

Wesley was afraid of the influence of the rich on others. At Dewsbury he notes that a change, for the worse, has come over the vicar who, from being deeply serious, had ceased because of his contacts with 'rich and honourable men, who soon cured him of that distraction'.[86] From time to time, however, he notes favourably the rich, as at Alnmouth when he says the two richest men had done all in their power to forward a Society.[87] At other times, he does not despair of the wealthy, remarking at York, that many of the 'rich and honourable' (a favourite phrase) crowded into the meetings, 'and is not "God able, even of these stones, to raise up children to Abraham?"'[88] He gladly notes at Gwennap (Cornwall), a little later, that there is a rich man who is old and not covetous.[89] When the rich attend his sermons and listen attentively, he gladly comments upon it, but with a

[83] ibid., p. 454.
[84] ibid., III.461.
[85] ibid., p. 479.
[86] ibid., IV.17.
[87] ibid., p. 27.
[88] ibid., IV.66.
[89] ibid., p. 78.

head-shaking none the less. At Pocklington this happened, but how hardly shall the rich ' escape from " the desire of other things "! '[90] he sighed. One, Mary Lewen, he regards as a most unusual example of divine grace because she, although left a fortune of £600 per annum, yet became a thorough Christian.[91] In Ireland, several times he remarks on gentry who were Christians, according to his standard. At Londonderry, he found honourable men who were ' doers ' as well as ' hearers '.[92] It was otherwise in his observation on the late Earl of Charleville, who had no profit from his riches and whose son ' was literally overwhelmed by them '.[93]

In marked contrast is Wesley's attitude toward the poor. If he took a prejudiced view of the rich, the poor he certainly saw in the best light, and sometimes through rose-coloured spectacles, although his attitude of accurate observation led him to record occasions when he saw the rich responding to the demands of the Gospel, and to denounce, often enough, those who fell below it and were at the same time poor. The difference in his attitude toward the two classes turns on his expectations. He did not expect a rich man to over-master the downward pull of his wealth, whereas he did expect the poor to find their poverty often a positive help toward their acceptance of the Christian life, and he shows little awareness of the dangers of poverty to Christian life. It would have been instructive to have had his comment upon the view of Richard Baxter, a man with whom he had much in common, who said: ' While pinching wants are calling away your mind . . . when there is a family to provide

[90] ibid., V.58.
[91] ibid., V.68.
[92] ibid., p. 205.
[93] ibid., p. 214.

for, a discontented wife and children to satisfy, rents and debts, and demands unpaid, it must be an excellent Christian that can live contentedly, and cast all his useless care on God. . . . Do the best to save the poor from such temptations, as you would yourselves be saved from them.'[94] Undoubtedly, Wesley would have agreed with the injunction at the end, but Baxter's earlier words would have failed to win much sympathy, for in a sermon he says: 'I have not known three-score rich persons, perhaps not half the number, during three-score years, who, as far as I can judge, were not less holy than they would have been had they been poor.'[95] The possession of wealth made people less tractable, less meek, and more impatient, Wesley argued. He recounts a visit he paid to a God-fearing baronet who gave away nine-tenths of his yearly income. A servant, putting coal on the fire in the room in which they were sitting, caused a puff of smoke to come out. The baronet petulantly exclaimed: 'O Mr. Wesley, these are the crosses I meet with daily.' Wesley's comment is characteristic and revealing: 'Would he not have been less impatient, if he had had fifty, instead of five thousand pounds a year?'[96] It is, perhaps, not without significance that Wesley did not marry until middle age, and then married a widow with a private income (this income Wesley did not touch, but he certainly did not have to make financial provision for his wife), so that, in fact, he had no personal knowledge of the anxieties of the poor man with a needy family. True, as we have seen, he was brought up under the almost constant shadow of want and debts, but important as that is, it does not quite put him in the position of a

[94] *How to do Good to Many* (*Works*, XVII.303).
[95] *Sermons*, II.310.
[96] *Arminian Magazine* (1781), I.79.

father of a hungry family. He had no love of poverty for its own sake but he thoroughly appreciated, and probably over-estimated, its usefulness in turning a man toward God.

We find him in Georgia days, noticing with approval the diligence of the poor at a place called Ebenezer,[97] but it is after his return to England that his mission stands out as primarily one to the poor, for in Georgia he was a parish priest in fact, although he had gone out with the special desire of being a missionary. At a period when it was popular to denounce the poor as idle good-for-nothings, Wesley adopted a very different view. He would visit, especially in London, the poorest of the poor, and records his experience of finding them in underground hovels and in garrets, ' half-starved both with cold and hunger, added to weakness and pain. But I found not one of them unemployed who was able to crawl about the room. So wickedly, devilishly false is that common objection, " They are poor only because they are idle ". ' He characteristically points the moral of this to those better off: ' If you saw these things with your own eyes, could you lay out money in ornaments or superfluities ? ' Ten days later (it was in March 1753) he visits more of the sick poor and is astonished at their industry, even though some of them could hardly move with illness, cold, and hunger.[98] He preferred always to minister to the poor, and if he had his way would always preach to them.[99] Over and over again, in his *Journal*, Wesley refers appreciatively to the poor in his congregations.

Having noted Wesley's attitude toward the rich and the poor respectively, we must now trace his importance in

[97] *Journal*, I.396.
[98] ibid., IV.52, 54.
[99] ibid., p. 358.

charitable work. Nehemiah Curnock, the editor of his *Journal*, points out that the young John Wesley was absorbed in his pursuit of holiness without at first any serious appreciation of that element in it of service for others, but that at Oxford this was corrected, and that later, in Georgia, this impulse received further encouragement.[100] It has already been remarked above that at Oxford Wesley started his charitable work amongst the prisoners, the poor, and the sick, and to this end he denuded himself even of what are commonly regarded as necessaries.[101] This was the beginning. For the rest of his life, after his evangelical conversion in 1738, he was constantly engaging in charitable enterprise, and spurring others to the same. Most of this work was of the *ad hoc* sort rather than proceeding from any fixed plan. Thus, preaching at Hanham, Bristol, in January 1740, Wesley noticed that many were unemployed on account of the severe frost then obtaining, and these had no relief from their parish. Accordingly, he made a collection, followed by two others, whereby he fed one hundred to one hundred and fifty persons a day.[102] The next winter, in London during November, he collects clothes for the 'numerous poor' of the society.[103] After these small experiences of relief in kind, later in the same month, Wesley considers with some of his followers several ways of helping the unemployed, and records, so characteristically: 'Our aim was, with as little expense as possible, to keep them at once from want and from idleness.' A dozen of the poorest were provided with employment in carding and spinning cotton for the winter months.

[100] ibid., 'Introductory', I.35.
[101] ibid., pp. 467–8.
[102] ibid., II.333.
[103] ibid., p. 399.

'And the design answered; they were employed and maintained with very little more than the produce of their own labour.'[104]

These experiences led him, in May 1741,[105] to propose to his United Society, in London, that a slightly more ambitious project should be undertaken. He reminds them that many of their brethren had not sufficient to eat and to wear; many were unemployed, 'without their own fault'; many were sick. He says that he has done all that his own resources in money made possible and it was not enough: therefore he proposes a scheme, that they should bring all their spare garments for distribution; give a penny a week for relief; and that he should employ unemployed women in knitting. 'To these we will first give the common price for what work they do; and then add, according as they need'—a combination of market price and charity. Then a dozen persons were to be appointed to inspect this work and also to visit and relieve the sick, and to meet weekly to report. Here is the true Wesley touch: charity without pauperization, freedom with disciplinary oversight. Visitation of the poor and the sick was a constant activity of Wesley for seventy years, and one which he trained others to do in all his Societies up and down the land. Frequently, he had collections for the poor at special services or on specially needful occasions, and these sums would be carefully laid out, often in kind, and distributed personally by Wesley or his helpers.[106] His activities in this direction were so numerous and became so well known, that there was a danger of rascals imitating the collecting, but for their own benefit.[107]

[104] ibid., pp. 403-4.
[105] ibid., II.453-4.
[106] cf. ibid., III.117, 122, 125, 281, 329.
[107] ibid., p. 365.

Another charitable device of Wesley was the founding of a 'lending-stock'. This began in 1746 and the method was to lend a pound at a time, to be repaid by weekly instalments within three months, chiefly for the benefit of small tradesmen.[108] Although this plan was never on a large scale it none the less proved a boon to a considerable number because it was continued over a long period; and we find Wesley urging it 'more strongly than ever I had done before' some twenty-odd years later.[109]

Charitable work begun, or inspired by Wesley, was not limited to Methodists, and an example of this is supplied by the 'Strangers' Friend Society', begun in London by one John Gardner. He wrote to Wesley to advise him of the project and obtain his help because of opposition: 'A few of us are subscribing a penny a week each, which is to be carried on the Sabbath by one of ourselves, who read and pray with the afflicted, who, according to the rules enclosed, must be poor strangers, having no parish, or friend at hand to help them. Our benevolent plan is opposed by my class-leader; therefore we are constrained to seek your approbation before we proceed. We are very poor, and our whole stock is not yet twenty shillings: will thank you, therefore, for any assistance you may please to afford your very humble servant.'[110] No explanation is offered as to why the class leader should oppose this scheme—it may have been due to some purely personal cause, or he may have felt there were enough poor within the Methodist ranks to absorb all the charitable impulses of their members. In any case, Wesley's reply was wholly approving, and to the point: 'I like the design and rules

---

[108] ibid., III.246, 329; *Letters*, II.309; *Wesley Historical Society Proceedings*, III.197–8; V.213.

[109] *Journal*, V.194.

[110] *Letters*, VII.308.

of your little Society and hope you will do good to many. I will subscribe threepence per week, and will give you a guinea in advance if you call on me Saturday morning.'[111]

This Society was begun in 1785, and in Bristol the following year. Wesley was not content merely to subscribe to such an object, but would want to find out for himself how it was working. He records that in March 1790 on a Sunday morning he 'met the Strangers' Society, instituted wholly for the relief, not of our society, but for poor, sick, friendless strangers. I do not know that I ever heard or read of such an institution till within a few years ago. So this also is one of the fruits of Methodism'.[112] Less than a month before he died, Wesley wrote a letter to Adam Clarke, and commends the latter for having started a similar Society.[113]

Wesley's importance in the field of charity lies in three directions, viz., his personal work in giving and in initiating charitable enterprises; his love for the poor, identification with them, and indirectly, in the new self-respect he gave them and the new life which often led to improved economic conditions for them; his insistence on the duty of poor-relief and employment for all who joined his Societies. It is the last of these which must now be considered, and it is this which is the most important.

Wesley directed his Societies from their inception in 1738 until his death in 1791, a period of over fifty-two years. During the whole of that time he was drumming into the minds of his followers two things in particular, First, that salvation was by faith and not in the least by works; second, that the saved man must live a life of love

[111] ibid.
[112] *Journal*, VIII.49.
[113] *Letters*, VIII.261.

which specifically included the relief of the sick and the poor. It was impossible for a member of a Methodist Society not to be aware of the religious importance (for himself) of charity, and also not to be made constantly aware of how this duty might be discharged. Poor-relief was not a side-line; on the contrary, it was inculcated with the strongest spiritual sanctions. Wesley once received a letter from a critic who had heard him preach (and who probably confused some of the rich hearers present with members of his Societies) and who criticized Methodists as not being sufficiently careful of their duty of charity. Wesley prints this critical letter and answers its charge that his followers were not sufficiently told of their duty by saying: ' I do tell them so: and I tell them it will be more tolerable in the day of judgement for Sodom and Gomorrah than for them. I tell them, the Methodists that do not fulfil all righteousness will have the hottest place in the lake of fire! '[114] Nor can one read his sermons without being aware of the truth of this refutation. Of course, it is true that some did not rise to the challenge of the poor as put to them, but many did. Of these was one who analyses his income and expenditure to show how of his £47 per annum he had succeeded in making his personal expenditure come down to under £28 per annum, the rest being given to the poor. He adds, much as Wesley himself would, ' And I think the poor themselves ought to be questioned with regard to drinking tea and beer. For I cannot think it right for them to indulge themselves in those things which I refrain from to help them.'[115] Tea was then very expensive, very much more so than the commonly drunk small beer.

It would be difficult to believe that this long continued

[114] *Journal*, V.240.
[115] ibid., 241–2.

training by Wesley in poor relief was without a considerable effect. Fortunately, we are to some extent able to quote figures in illustration, and even proof, for the account book of the Stewards of the Methodist Societies of London is still in existence. From this it appears that, to take a period, in the twenty years from 1770 to 1789, when the membership in London averaged about 2,560, there was given to the poor £14,999 8s. 10d. This is a remarkable figure when it is remembered that many of the membership were poor people themselves being helped out of this fund, and in addition much was given in kind. Furthermore, during these years large sums were spent on new buildings, the money being raised mostly on loan and without any diminution of the money for the poor on that account; and the only staple income of the Societies was the customary subscription of one penny per member per week and one shilling per quarter. Other expenditure by the Societies, during this time, included £11,245 5s. 7d. on the maintenance of 'Preachers and Families', a term which not only includes those working in London, but many outside, so that the cost of the Methodist ministry in London, and part of the cost of many up and down the land, is almost exactly seventy-five per cent of the sum contributed to the poor, an extraordinary figure.[116]

[116] See MS., 'Account of Cash receiv'd and disburs'd by the Society in London under ye direction of the Reverend Mr. John and Chas. Wesley, 1766–1803'. (Kept at the Methodist Book Room, City Road, London.) For a detailed analysis of the figures for this twenty-year period, see Bebb, op. cit., pp. 184–6 (Appendix 8).

Chapter Six
Wesley's Concern with Certain Economic Questions

WESLEY's love of the poor, and his tireless work in the cause of charity, together with his understanding of all possessions as constituting a stewardship from God, are parts of the same whole, which receives its clearest representation in his attitude toward money. Money he regarded as a valuable means toward the end of human happiness, but when not rightly used, as a great danger. These views were an amalgam of his observation of life— as shown particularly in his attitude toward the rich—and his understanding of the teaching of the Bible, strengthened by his own practice.

Wesley's detailed attitude toward money, and its rightful and wrongful use, comes out in two of his sermons, the first of which is from his series on the Sermon on the Mount (number eight in that series).[1] Here he urges the need for the same purity of motive in business as in devotions and alms-giving, so that a man cannot be said to be serving God in his employment, accepting his work as a vocation, if he labours simply to acquire more wealth and a higher position: 'For vain and earthly designs are no more allowable in our employments, than in our alms and devotions.' The person who seeks anything from the earth instead of doing all to the glory of God, will become full of ungodliness and unrighteousness. He will know no peace, and that applies both to the pursuit of wealth and its enjoyment, if he aims ' at anything beside God '. Accordingly, they were urged not to seek to accumulate wealth. Wesley then compares the ordinary ' Christian '

[1] *Sermons*, I.473–94.

Englishman unfavourably with the American Indian because the latter ' desires and seeks nothing more than plain food to eat, and plain raiment to put on; and he seeks this only from day to day: he reserves, he lays up nothing; unless it be as much corn at one season of the year as he will need before that season returns '. Whereas even those commonly regarded as good Christians, Wesley says, will get as much wealth as they can, and keep as much as they choose. Even though many of them may do so quite honestly, they are none the less committing a sin in seeking to acquire and retain wealth for their own enjoyment. This does not mean, however, that economic activity and enterprise are wrong. On the contrary, it is the duty of a man to provide for the reasonable wants of himself and his household, to pay his debts, and to provide a means of livelihood for his children for them to follow after he is gone. Wesley sees that this implies a measure of capital: ' We are not forbidden . . . to lay up, from time to time, what is needful for the carrying on our worldly business, in such a measure and degree as is sufficient to answer the foregoing purposes.'[2] In other words, business is allowable, but not ' big business'; saving is right, but not so that it makes possible living on investments. He then recapitulates, to avoid any danger of his meaning being missed, that what is wrong is striving after more wealth than is necessary for the real needs of a person and his family, together with some working capital—' a sufficiency to carry on his worldly business, so far as answers these reasonable purposes '. If he seeks more, then he is denying his Lord.

The next section of this sermon is invective and appeal mingled. In it unnecessary (according to Wesley's

[2] These rightful uses of money are frequently alluded to by Wesley, e.g. *Arminian Magazine* (1781), I.18.

definition of unnecessary) wealth is referred to as ' thick clay ', and the man who aims at it has ' murdered his own soul ', he has ' gained riches and hell-fire.[3] Anyone may observe for himself that those who covet money have failed to win happiness and have already anticipated the hell to which they are going! '

Wesley admits that it is not necessarily true that every rich man is bound for hell, for a man may be rich through no ' fault ' of his own—it may even be God's will for him, so that, dangerous as they undoubtedly are, riches do not inevitably ruin a man's soul. Where the soul is inevitably lost is where men *desire* wealth; such men are as Judas selling his Lord. To any who may be moved to escape the destruction their previous desire for wealth has brought near, Wesley says that they are not necessarily to get rid of their wealth, but to learn to look at wealth in a different way, so as to esteem it but ' dung and dross '. Also they should no longer trust in riches, neither for help nor happiness, nor seek to increase their wealth further. On the contrary, use wealth as a wise steward, not indeed throwing it away, but distributing to the needy, after one's household has been maintained. There are always the hungry, ill-clothed, sick, and the prisoners needing help.

We come now to that famous sermon on the ' Use of Money '[4] in which Wesley gives the most detailed conspectus of his attitude toward the right use of money (the sermon above analysed being much more on the wrong use of money). Wesley appears first to have preached

[3] Wesley could not fairly be described as a hell-fire preacher, although he did sometimes preach about it. When he did so, the appeal or attack was usually directed toward the rich, or the would-be rich, as when he found a number of rich people in the congregation he would deliver his sermon on Dives and Lazarus.

[4] *Sermons*, II.311–27.

this sermon in 1744, and at the service the collection was given to providing bread and clothing for the needy. The sermon is mentioned in his Sermon Register no less than twenty-two times, and was first published in 1760, but much of what is in it was preached in other connexions again and again. The truth is that these sermons represent a cycle of ideas which, as the very numerous comments on the rich in his *Journal* make plain, were never far from his preaching. The right use of his money, Wesley saw as a pungent test of a man's Christianity, while the consequences of its wrongful use were often employed by him as a means of arousing the conscience. This sermon was preached on Luke 16[9]: ' I say unto you, Make to yourselves friends of the mammon of unrighteousness; that, when ye fail, they may receive you into everlasting habitations.'

He begins by a reference to the Scriptural context, explains that ' Mammon ' means riches or money, and then complains that Christians do not sufficiently consider the use of ' this excellent talent ', i.e. money, the introduction of which into the world he regards as an instance of God's wise providence. After all, it is the love of money, not the thing itself, which is the root of all evil. Its value as an international instrument, and as a social medium, is immense. Money, rightly used, means food, clothing, and shelter to those needing them. It can defend the oppressed, and be the means of bringing health to the sick. Therefore it is of the utmost importance that the Christian should know how properly to use this excellent gift of God, and this proper use may be condensed into three precepts, viz. Gain all you can; Save all you can; and, Give all you can. Wesley's understanding of what is comprised by the first of these three precepts is instructive. He deduces from it that it is a positive duty not to pay for a thing more than it is worth, nor to continue a day longer than is necessary in an employment dangerous to health, dangerous either on account of its nature or of the excessive hours of labour. He instances occupations giving rise to lead poisoning as a case of one dangerous by its nature, and also a post which, for a person of weak constitution, involved too long hours of working. The underlying principle here is that life is more important than livelihood. Similarly, occupations injurious to a healthy outlook ('a healthful mind') should be avoided as much as those bodily injurious. Such occupations are those which a man cannot properly be engaged in without detriment to his conscience, such as smuggling, or such businesses as involved trickery to so great an extent that it was impossible to pursue them honestly. Then there is another class of occupation which, although not injurious either to body or mind in itself, may do its practitioners great harm because in it they must associate with evil company. To these, Wesley quaintly adds, such occupations as may have bad results on a particular individual although not evil in themselves, explaining that he, for instance, could not study mathematics to any advanced degree 'without being a Deist, if not an Atheist', an allowance for the personal equation.

Similarly, our duty to gain all we can must involve no harm to others, such as may happen through gambling, overcharging, or exacting too high a rate of interest which excludes, Wesley says, all pawnbroking. He recognizes that there is a case to be made out for the pawnbroker, that his activities may sometimes be beneficial, but it is an occupation which 'all unprejudiced men see with grief to be abundantly overbalanced by the evil'. No doubt, Wesley felt pawnbroking to be an encouragement to thriftlessness and to an attitude the reverse of stewardship. Also, in pursuing the aim of gaining all one can, one ought not to hurt one's neighbour by underselling him with a view to capturing his trade, nor, of course, attempt to get from him his prized workmen. Nor may one hurt others in their body, which, according to Wesley, excludes all traffic in spirits, except as required for medicinal purposes. He then illustrates his point by denouncing those doctors who, he alleges, do not cure their patients as quickly as possible, in order to get more fees. And finally, under this heading, he warns against doing anything in business which will hurt another's soul, by ministering to immorality or intemperance. Therefore, he calls on all licenced victuallers and providers of amusements to consider the effects of their activities which may, or may not, hurt the souls of others.

These provisos apart, every man should strive to gain all he can. This demands application—no time to be wasted, no pains spared to understand the technique of the business concerned, no procrastination, no halfhearted effort. On the contrary, every effort should be made to improve business methods, it being a shame for the Christian not to outdo in business efficiency and initiative the non-Christian, and that because the Christian should be putting more energy into his work, while suffering less from worldly distractions.

The next thing, having made all the profit one legitimately can, is to save as much as possible. Therefore do not waste money in superfluous expenditure in respect of food or furniture. Let no money be spent in ways calculated to gain the admiration of others. Nor should money be spent unnecessarily on one's children any more than on oneself. Then follows a strong admonition to parents not to leave their children a large amount of money if they have any doubts as to the good use which the children would make of it. As a deduction from this comes the further point, that if one child had a proper (i.e. a religious) valuation of money then it should be mostly left to him, even if he should be the younger. In cases where parents recognize that none of their children can be relied upon to use wealth properly, then they should each be left only such money as would enable them to live at the standard to which they have been accustomed,[5] and the remainder disposed of so as to do the most good with it. But Wesley admits that this last injunction is unlikely to be obeyed.

Then comes the climax: 'Give all you can!' Money saved must be properly used, otherwise it may as well be thrown away. Wesley did not appreciate fully the function of the Bank, for he says that to put money in the Bank of England, and leave it there, was the same as burying it.[6] The attitude and duty of stewardship is then enforced once more; men are to realize that their substance is God's to be employed as He will, which, said Wesley, admits of no doubt. They should first provide for their own households and then assist other Christians ('the household of faith'), and what remains should be used for any others. To act in this way, carefully and conscientiously, is to give all 'not only by what you give to the poor, but also by that which you expend in providing things needful for yourself and your household'. If one is in doubt whether he ought to expend a particular sum on himself or his family, then let him consider his proposed expenditure seriously as a Christian; if still in doubt, let

[5] This might, of course, mean leaving a child quite an amount of wealth. Wesley does not object to that, probably holding the view that provided the child has always been used to that standard of living it was no more likely to be spiritually dangerous than a lower standard.

[6] Banking business had not by this time developed in the way that it has done since.

him resort to prayer. Finally comes the challenge: 'Act up to the dignity of your calling! No more sloth! Whatsoever your hand findeth to do, do it with your might! No more waste! Cut off every expense which fashion, caprice, or flesh and blood demand! No more covetousness! But employ whatever God has entrusted you with, in doing good, all possible good, in every possible kind and degree, to the household of faith, to all men!'

Such a sermon, the substance of which was often repeated, naturally raised much opposition, one form of which was the challenge to Wesley that he did not practise what he preached in this connexion. He takes up the challenge and replies:[7] 'Permit me to speak as freely of myself, as I would of another man. I *gain all I can* (namely by writing) without hurting either my soul or body. I *save all I can*, not willingly wasting any thing. . . . Yet by *giving all I can*, I am effectually secured from *laying up treasures upon earth*. Yea, and I am secured from either desiring or endeavouring it, as long as I *give all I can*. . . . But some may say, " Whether you endeavour it or no, you are undeniably *rich*. You have more than the necessaries of life." I have. . . . Two and forty years ago, having a desire to furnish poor people with cheaper, shorter, and plainer books than any I had seen, I wrote many small tracts, generally a penny a-piece; and afterwards several larger. Some of these had such a sale as I never thought of; and by this means I unawares became rich. But I never desired or endeavoured after it. And now that it is come upon me unawares, I lay up no treasures upon earth: I lay up nothing at all. My desire, and endeavour in this respect is, to " wind my bottom round the year ". I cannot help leaving my books behind me, whenever God calls me hence. But in every

[7] *Arminian Magazine* (1781) I.74–5.

other respect, my own hands will be my executors.'
That Wesley succeeded in this is well known; he left
practically no estate, except his writings.

Wesley was no economist, yet a claim may reasonably
be made that he was not without significance in modern
English economic history. For he had much to do with
those classes of people who were of importance in the new
economy which the advent of the Industrial Revolution
was gradually putting in place of the time-honoured
economy based upon land and upon wool. And over
these people his influence was greater than that of any
other single individual. His injunctions to them in respect
of economic activities were religious and ethical, but they
were accompanied by the habit of economic observation.
He not only told workmen, small traders, and merchants,
how they ought to act in respect of their time and money,
but he was well aware of the contemporary conditions of
trade and industry. This is of importance because they
must feel that he was not only a Christian idealist of the
most rigorous sort, but also one who knew actual conditions, and therefore they would be the more ready to
listen. It may also be added that he spoke with that
prestige which always attaches to the successful; in
business affairs, whether to do with the marketing of his
books, or the financial side of his Societies and Chapels, he
showed his acumen and ability.

The habit of economic observation was well established
with him, for while still in Georgia he took his opportunities in this direction and made notes at considerable
length. Soon after his return to England, he made a long
report of these matters to the Trustees for Georgia,
describing in detail the economic geography of Georgia,
its natural resources, fertility, and yields of various crops,
possibilities through good drainage, state of the main

plantations, together with an estimate of the economic life and possibilities of the Indians in and around that Colony.[8] In his German visit, Wesley notes the industrial discipline at the Herrnhut settlement: ' As it behoves all Christians not to be slothful in business, but diligently to attend the works of their calling, there are persons chosen by the Church to superintend all those who are employed in outward business. And by this means also many things are prevented which might otherwise be an occasion of offence.'[9]

During his long evangelistic career, Wesley records places and times where trade is either good or bad, sometimes adapting his preaching accordingly. For example, at Norwich in 1772: ' Finding abundance of people were out of work, and consequently, in the utmost want (such a general decay of trade having hardly been known in the memory of man), I enforced, in the evening: " Seek ye first the kingdom of God, and His righteousness; and all these things shall be added unto you." For many years I have not seen so large a congregation here, in the mornings as well as evenings. One reason of which may be this: thousands of people who, when they had fullness of bread, never considered whether they had any souls or not, now they are in want begin to think of God.'[10] Here at Norwich he shows his general attitude that economic affairs are also religious affairs. This means not only that Christian ethics must be brought to bear upon economic aims and practices, but also that questions of providence and prayer were relevant to economic situations. So he can preach to a large hungry congregation on seeking first the kingdom of God, being quite sure that

[8] *Journal*, I.401–6, 439.
[9] ibid., II.53.
[10] ibid., V.486.

then the other things, bread and other necessaries, would be forthcoming. We see the same point of view in his reaction to the situation at the end of that year and the beginning of 1773, when in London:[11] 'Being greatly embarrassed by the necessities of the poor, we spread all our wants before God in solemn prayer; believing that He would sooner "make windows in heaven" than suffer His truth to fail.' This is followed eight days later by observing a day of fasting and prayer 'on account of the general want of trade and scarcity of provisions'.

In 1776, in the course of an extensive tour, Wesley carefully notes the economic conditions.[12] He says: 'In travelling through Berkshire, Oxfordshire, Bristol, Gloucestershire, Worcestershire, Warwickshire, Staffordshire, Cheshire, Lancashire, Yorkshire, Westmorland, and Cumberland, I diligently made two inquiries. The first was concerning the increase or decrease of the people; the second concerning the increase or decrease of trade. As to the latter, it is, within these last two years, amazingly increased; in several branches in such a manner as has not been known in the memory of man. Such is the fruit of the entire civil and religious liberty which all England now enjoys! And as to the former, not only in every city and large town, but in every village and hamlet, there is no decrease, but a very large and swift increase. One sign of this is the swarms of little children which we see in every place.' This improvement in economic conditions, since 1772, he notes to be in evidence elsewhere as well, for in London, in 1778, he remarks,[13] with some surprise: 'I . . . found a surprising difference in their worldly circumstances. Five or six years ago, one in three among the lower ranks of people was out of employment, and the case

[11] ibid., pp. 495–6. [12] ibid., VI.104.
[13] ibid., p. 180.

was supposed to be nearly the same through all London and Westminster. I did not now, after all the tragical outcries of want of trade that fill the nation, find one in ten out of business; nay, scarce one in twenty, even in Spitalfields.'

Nor did Wesley only observe and preach; he also, in pamphlets and letters contributed to discussion of economic difficulties and changes, and questions of poverty and under-nourishment. In his *Thoughts on the Present Scarcity of Provisions*, a pamphlet of 1773,[14] he attempts to generalize on the actual conditions he had seen at Norwich, London, and elsewhere. He argues that the situation is largely the result of high taxation, increased rents, and the general rise in the cost of living. Bread, in particular, was dear because too high a proportion of 'bread-corn' was used for distilling. Luxury, he argued, was another cause of high prices generally.

Five years later, in 1778, he published another tract corresponding to the altered conditions he had observed in his tours: *A Serious Address to the People of England, with Regard to the State of the Nation*.[15] In this, he points to the improved conditions of the multitude and the increase in population, and desiring people to be calm and contented and not to give way to the state of excitement prevalent in the nation at the time. Wesley's importance from the economic standpoint does not depend upon his economic arguments, which were far from being always sound, for he was no trained economist. But he was a trained observer, and he was a stabilizing force in a period of considerable economic change, the causes of which, and the outcome of which, were understood by few. Always the enemy of panic, he helped not a little to preserve nerve and balance in the minds of many at that time.

[14] Published in *Wesley's Works*, XI.53ff.   [15] See ibid., pp. 140ff.

Chapter Seven

The Influence of a Man Deeply Concerned

AN ENDEAVOUR has been made above to indicate Wesley's religious teaching and his social and economic concern, and to observe the way in which the one impinged upon the other. The question now arises as to his effectiveness in this direction. Modern historians tend to emphasize the importance of Wesley as a social factor,[1] but is it possible to do more than express a judgement arrived at after a study of Wesley's writing and his life, a judgement which, however carefully considered, remains a personal view? What is needed, if it can be obtained, is an objective criterion, itself based upon factual data. The influence of any great preacher or writer is never easy to investigate in this way except in any particular matter over which his work may have been decisive in causing change, in the law or in some definite social custom. Nevertheless, there are objective data which, although not finally determinative, will enable the student to base his judgement on something more than a personal impression. These are principally two, viz., the numbers of his adherents and the discipline he exercised. It must be insisted that neither of these can be exactly measured, but both are susceptible of objective analysis.

John Wesley began his evangelical ministry in 1738 and in a few months' time the pattern of the Methodist Societies was taking shape, but naturally it was years before anything of a statistical nature was sought or

[1] Amongst them are H. W. V. Temperley in the *Cambridge Modern History*, Halévy in his work, *A History of the English People in 1815*, and specialist writers such as Maldwyn Edwards, J. S. Simon and Warner.

available. It was not, in fact, until the 1760s that figures for the Societies as a more or less organized body appear. We find that thirty years after Wesley began, in 1768, there were forty circuits and 27,341 members; ten years later, sixty circuits and 40,089 members; twenty years later, ninety-nine circuits and 66,375 members. In another ten years, in 1798, when Wesley had been dead for seven years, the number had risen to one hundred and forty-nine circuits with 101,712 members.[2]

It is true that we cannot be certain of the absolute accuracy of these figures; indeed, they are sometimes wrongly totalled in the original printed copy of the Minutes, yet there is no reason to doubt their substantial accuracy for they are confirmed to some extent by the story of the growth of Methodism revealed in the *Journal*.[3] We cannot reliably compare these figures, decade by decade, with the figures for the population of the country as a whole because the first census was not taken until 1801 and a considerable increase of population had already taken place during the previous half-century. We can only say in this regard, that soon after Wesley died there were just about 100,000 members of Methodist Societies in a total population of about nine million. This gives only one Methodist to every ninety of the

[2] Compiled from the *Minutes of the Methodist Conferences from the First, held in London, by the late Rev. John Wesley, A.M., in the year 1744*—the 1812 and 1862 editions, the latter edition having various alterations and additions.

[3] They also receive some confirmation in a polemical anti-Methodist work of the period, published anonymously, entitled *Enthusiasm of Methodists and Papists Compared*. In Part 2, Vol. I, p. 2, it says: 'What first occurs to my thoughts is the boasted success of their preaching, proved by the numbers of their followers, and converts. Here they triumph beyond measure: and perhaps not without some degree of foundation. For considering how inconsiderate and injudicious, how unlearned and unstable a large portion of mankind is this growth in numbers, grudgingly admitted, is alleged to be not surprising.'

population, but such a proportion would be most misleading, the following factors having to be taken into account.

First, whereas the population figures include all—men, women, and children—those of Methodism include only adults, and that at a time when large families were common, and when the expectation of life was relatively short, so that the proportion of adults to children may have been no more than one third, in which case we get one Methodist to every thirty adults of the population. Secondly, these statistics of Methodists refer only to Society members and do not include 'adherents', those who were influenced by Methodism, attended its public services, accepted its outlook, and largely its standards, but who did not become Class members. There is no means of attaining a scientific estimate of these people, yet the experience of most religious bodies encourages the supposition that a conservative estimate would equate the number of adherents to the number of members. Thirdly, the influence of Wesley on members of other religious bodies would appear to have been fairly considerable toward the later part of his life. Earlier on, both the Established Church and the dissenting bodies were for the most part antipathetic, but later there developed in both an Evangelical section which owed much to the inspiration of John Wesley. It is clear, however, that it is the figure of one Methodist to about every thirty adults of the population which is our only approach to an objective datum, but these other considerations will encourage us to believe that this figure is, in fact, an underestimate.

The question now arises as to what extent the social outlook of Wesley, based upon his religious ideas, impressed itself upon the members of his Societies. Here we are not left to flounder on opinions as to his probable effectiveness as a preacher and as a writer, because of the remarkable comprehension and forcefulness of his discipline. The Methodist church discipline of the eighteenth century has no parallel in modern English ecclesiastical history. It is not too much to say that it would be regarded as intolerable by almost all members of any Christian communion in this country to-day. It had two main sources: Wesley's own most unusual desire to be criticized ruthlessly, and his deep sense of responsibility before God for his followers which made him determined to take the most complete steps to see that his message not only went home, but was effective in daily life. He pursued holiness, for himself and others, and for this, discipline, both self-discipline and that of the members of the body, was felt to be indispensable. As a youth he would write home asking not only for advice but more than advice, and that at an age when most young people do not relish it. He would lay his own personal affairs, even the most intimate, such as his successive love affairs, before others for their judgement, while all his life he took it as a real favour to be dealt with ' home ', as he called hard criticism. He had almost a morbid love of this kind of thing, as though without it he might fail in the pursuit of holiness. On one occasion a certain Mr. Horton told him that he liked nothing about him and that his sermons were only personal satires and that no one could make head or tail of what religion it was Wesley had. Wesley's comment was: ' He was too warm for hearing an answer. So I had nothing to do but to thank him for his openness, and walk away.'[4] Another using these words might well be suspected of sarcasm, but Wesley's thanks for his critic's

[4] *Journal*, I.234.

'openness' were genuine. Occasionally, his preachers would round on him with criticism, even bitter criticism, but always it was received not merely with meekness but with gratitude. And what he practised himself he made others practise.

The rules of Methodist discipline appeared from the first, and were enlarged and amended time and time again. Moreover, we find this discipline concerned much more with social and moral faults than with ecclesiastical. As early as the 25th December 1738, some seven months only after his conversion experience, he drew up the 'Rules of the Band Societies'.[5] Under these, every person who wished to join a Methodist Band had these questions, amongst others, put to him: 'Do you desire to be told of all your faults, and that plain and home? ... Consider! Do you desire we should tell you whatsoever we think, whatsoever we fear, concerning you? Do you desire that, in doing this, we should come as close as possible, that we should cut to the quick, and search your heart to the bottom?'[6] What all this would involve, in the regimentation of life, appeared clearly six years later with the issue of Wesley's 'Directions given to the Band Societies'. In them he writes: 'You are supposed to have the faith that "overcometh the world". To you, therefore, it is not grievous, Carefully to abstain from doing evil: in particular (*inter alia*) To taste no spirituous liquor, no dram of any kind, unless prescribed by a physician; To be at a word both in buying and selling; To pawn nothing, no, not to save life; To wear no needless ornaments, such as rings, ear-rings; ... To use

---

[5] At the Fetter Lane Society, Disciplinary Rules, most probably the work of Wesley himself, were adopted at the beginning of May 1738—i.e. before Wesley's evangelical conversion.

[6] Wesley's *Works*, VIII.272–3.

no needless self-indulgence, such as taking snuff or tobacco. . . . To give alms of such things as you possess, and that to the uttermost of your power. To be patterns of diligence and frugality, of self-denial, and taking up the cross daily.'[7] The 'Rules of the United Societies' were very similar.

Nothing was too small, upon occasion, to be made a matter of discipline, and that discipline was to be exercised, in the first instance, by the Band or Class leader and other members, that is, by those who saw one's life day by day. In the next instance, it was exercised by the preachers and the Assistant,[8] and finally by Wesley himself. He is usually thought of as a constantly moving itinerant evangelist, but he was no less a constantly moving judge, and court of appeal, in respect of discipline. Inevitably, the exercise of this discipline was not uniform, for a great deal depended upon the Assistant, not always a man of character strong enough to enforce it, and sometimes himself needing (and in due course receiving) correction. But every Assistant knew that presently, in the course of his tours, Wesley would come again and demand to meet the Bands, and to go through the list of members, name by name, making the most searching inquiries. Nothing is more striking in the *Journal* of John Wesley that the almost innumerable occasions when he notes: 'I examined the Societies' or, more suggestive still, 'I regulated the Societies', while over and over again he states that he read and explained the Rules. Then, when necessary, the discipline would be executed and some members would be excluded. This exclusion meant that no quarterly membership ticket would be

[7] ibid., pp. 273–4.

[8] This term 'Assistant' is somewhat misleading. By it Wesley means one who assisted him by being his local representative in a circuit and better described by the modern term now employed, viz. 'Superintendent'.

issued, and so the person concerned would not be able to gain admission to Band or Society meeting (they could still of course, like anyone else, attend the public preaching services). This must also have involved a social stigma, but it was often felt to be more than that, for in the eyes of many the quarterly ticket was not only a passport to the meeting, but to heaven. The frequent practice of early Methodists of having their membership tickets buried with them strongly suggests a certain superstitious belief that it was good to carry into the grave documentary evidence of their salvation.[9]

To give a complete account of all the instances recorded by Wesley himself of his disciplinary action, and oversight, would be a major undertaking, but reference must be made to a number to show the widespread character of this discipline, both in regard to time, places, and uniformity. To start with Bristol, one of Wesley's three main centres, we see the method and results of a typical disciplinary inquiry, and for which Wesley's own words will give the best picture. Tuesday 24th February 1741: ' The Bands meeting at Bristol, I read over the names of the United Society, being determined that no disorderly walker should remain therein. Accordingly I took account of every person (1) to whom any reasonable objection was made; (2) who was not known to and recommended by some on whose veracity I could depend. To those who were sufficiently recommended, tickets were given on the following days. Most of the rest I had face to face with their accusers; and such as either appeared to be innocent, or confessed their faults and promised better behaviour, were then received into the Society. The others were put upon trial again, unless they voluntarily

---

[9] This practice is noted by Sydney G. Dimond, *The Psychology of the Methodist Revival*, p. 221.

expelled themselves. About forty were by this means separated from us; I trust only for a season.'[10] Later, the same year, he records, after inquiry, removing all those from the Societies in London 'whose behaviour or spirit was not agreeable to the gospel of Christ'.[11] John Wesley firmly believed in the advantages of a small number of members keen in their profession and conduct over a larger number of less reliable people. In a letter, written to 'Tommy' (? Thomas Rankin, one of the preachers) in the year 1764, and published recently for the first time, he says: 'The old Proverb says, Half is more than ye whole. Certainly Half the People who called themselves a Society, well united together are better than twice as many, who are only as a rope of Sand.'[12]

Discipline was exercised under Wesley by Class leaders. The organization into Classes began in Bristol, and was instituted in London in the Spring of 1742. In the latter place he 'appointed several earnest and sensible men to meet me, to whom I showed the great difficulty I had long found of knowing the people who desired to be under my care. After much discourse, they all agreed there could be no better way to come to a sure, thorough knowledge of each person than to divide them into Classes, like those at Bristol, under the inspection of those in whom I could most confide. This was the origin of our Classes at London, for which I can never sufficiently praise God, the unspeakable usefulness of the institution having ever since been more and more manifest.'[13] At the same time, also in London, he was 'constrained' to exclude some

[10] *Journal*, II.429–30.
[11] ibid., pp. 518–19.
[12] *Wesley Historical Society Proceedings* (December 1943), p. 59.
[13] *Journal*, II.535.

'who did not show their faith by their works'.[14] There was nothing perfunctory in these examinations of Societies, and frequently Wesley records that he spent several days on this task in only one place.[15] Always, he felt a deep responsibility for every individual with whom he was concerned, and this did not lessen with the years. He would sometimes say he could not understand how any minister could ever face the account of his stewardship of souls unless he knew by name every member.[16] Sometimes the expulsions would be numerous, almost wholesale, as when in Newcastle, in February 1743, after an investigation lasting a week, over fifty out of eight hundred odd were excommunicated.[17] Nearly always, these disciplinary visitations were accompanied by the reading and expounding of the searching Rules. At a village called Chowden, in the North of England, Wesley does this, desiring 'everyone seriously to consider whether he was willing to conform thereto or no. That this would shake many of them I knew well'.[18] It did. Wesley expels sixty-four persons there, and gives the reasons, the social character of most of which is very illuminating, viz.: 2 were expelled for cursing; 2 for habitual Sabbath-breaking; 17 for drunkenness; 2 for selling spirits; 3 for quarrelling; 1 for wife-beating; 3 for habitual lying; 4 for 'railing and evil-speaking'; 1 for idleness; and 29 for 'lightness and carelessness'.[19] It will be noted that few were expelled for strictly religious faults, and none for doctrinal differences, while significantly enough, the largest number were excluded for not taking seriously

[14] ibid., III.39.
[15] e.g. ibid., p. 49.
[16] e.g. ibid., p. 65.
[17] ibid., p. 67.
[18] ibid., p. 68.
[19] ibid., p. 71.

enough their religion, and to take it seriously always involved, in Wesley's view, right conduct to one's neighbour.

In Bristol, in the autumn of 1743, Wesley spends several days in ' purging ' the Society,[20] while on his next period in London he actually spent some weeks ' in speaking severally to the members of the Society. Many of these I was obliged to set aside: there remained about two and twenty hundred persons '.[21] In 1748, we find him reducing the numbers of the Bristol Society from 900 to 730, no fewer than 170 being expelled.[22] Here was pastoral oversight at its most rigorous. At Nottingham, in 1746, he decided that the condition of the Society there was such that he would deal drastically, so he ' made short work, cutting off . . . at a stroke, and leaving only that little handful who . . . were really in earnest '.[23] A significant insight is obtained from a letter Wesley received from a Class leader who, at Wesley's request, made his account of those under his care. The letter starts: ' I hope my Class are bending one way.' He then goes on to mention them one by one, under their initials, grouping them as he thinks their state of life warrants.[24] In Dublin, the following year, after examining the Society, Wesley notes that they are of a very teachable spirit, but adds, characteristically, that this only means that they must be ' watched over with the more care, being equally susceptible of good and ill impressions '.[25]

[20] ibid., p. 97.
[21] ibid., p. 113.
[22] ibid., p. 380.
[23] ibid., p. 237.
[24] ibid., pp. 276–7. The writer of this letter, John Hague, concludes: ' It seems to me we all want advice that is plain and cutting, awakening and shaking, and hastening us. . . . May He give us to feel the true state of our souls! '
[25] ibid., p. 314.

The struggle against smuggling involved the exercise of disciplinary powers. In Cornwall, at St. Ives, in 1753, Wesley records that he began to examine the Society but soon had to stop short because he found that almost all were buying or selling goods which had not paid the duties on them, so he ' told them plain, either they must put this abomination away, or they would see my face no more ', which meant that the whole Society would be excommunicated.[26] At Portsmouth Common, he found people, who had awakened spiritually under Methodist preaching, meeting in a Society, but he refused to take any ' account ' of this Society which he called a ' shadow ' because they had no knowledge of the Rules. So the Rules were explained, and those willing to abide by them were gathered into a new Society.[27] These disciplinary investigations involved the respective duties of husbands and wives, and so extended into the intimate home life of the people.[28]

At Neath, in 1758, he returns to find the Society there ' an unlicked mass ', and suitably deals with them.[29] At Sunderland, another area notable for its smugglers and those profiting by their activities, Wesley spoke to each member of the Society, and adds: ' Most of the robbers, commonly called smugglers, have left us; but more than twice the number of honest people are already come in their place. And if none had come, yet should I not dare to keep those who steal either from the King or subject.'[30] At Norwich, in 1761, account is taken of the Society, ' but many of them were as bullocks unaccustomed to the yoke.

[26] ibid., IV.76.
[27] ibid., p. 84.
[28] ibid., p. 259.
[29] ibid., p. 284.
[30] ibid., p. 325.

Where or what will they be a year hence?'[31] Two years later, there is trouble at Norwich again, as there frequently was. He decides to try them one year more, i.e. if their conduct is not more satisfactory then, he will disband the whole.[32] Back in Bristol, in 1764, he is engaged in 'narrowly' examining the members one by one because he has heard that there were 'disorderly walkers' amongst them.[33]

Often the discipline was preventive, that is, Wesley would endeavour to forestall future expulsions by warning people, not only by the reading of the Rules, but by direct exhortation with regard to things that were likely to cause trouble. An illustration of this is at Londonderry where he exhorted the Society ' to avoid sloth, prodigality, and sluttishness, and, on the contrary, to be patterns of diligence, frugality, and cleanliness'.[34] Sometimes, he is able gladly to acknowledge that no exclusions are necessary, and remarks at Dover in 1765 that now smuggling has ceased there, the whole aspect is changed for the better.[35]

The same discipline was exacted of the children, at Kingswood and other Methodist schools, although he found his troubles in the schools constantly recurring, sometimes because of the children and at other times because of the staff. In 1766, he is determined to act finally, and spoke to masters, to servants, and to children: ' I will kill or cure: I will have one or the other—a Christian school, or none at all.'[36] Similarly with any other groups within the Methodist polity, for, when next

[31] ibid., p. 432.
[32] ibid., V.36.
[33] ibid., p. 98.
[34] ibid., p. 118.
[35] ibid., p. 151.
[36] ibid., p. 159.

at Londonderry he found the choir had, through the neglect of proper oversight on the part of the preacher concerned, become lax, so he meets them 'for the last time'.[37]

In Wales, as well as in England and Ireland, the same control was exercised. In 1774, at Pembroke, Wesley finds the Society in a 'languid state', and this he attributes to the absence of discipline which had, he says, been a feature there for some time, but this state of affairs he now rectifies.[38] At Colchester, a few years later, he not only visits the people individually but 'divided the Classes anew, which had been strangely and irregularly jumbled together (he insisted on separate Classes for married and for single, for men and for women); appointed stewards; regulated temporal and well as spiritual things'.[39] At York, in 1786, Wesley is pleased at the healthy state of the Society, and he ascribes this as due principally to the 'exact' discipline long in vogue there.[40] There is no remission of the work of enforcing Methodist discipline even when he is in advanced years. We find him, at 84 years of age, in Dublin, spending six days in visiting the various Classes and then excluding no less than one hundred and twelve members.[41] Thus to the end it goes on, so that, however lax one part or another might get, presently Wesley would appear and his unbending will be set to supply what was lacking. Here we have in the midst of a country in which a considerable amount of lawlessness existed, an ever-growing body of people governed according to strict principles from a central source. The result was that a mechanism existed whereby

[37] ibid., p. 419.
[38] ibid., VI.36.
[39] ibid., p. 377.
[40] ibid., VII.160.
[41] ibid., p. 294.

THE INFLUENCE OF A MAN DEEPLY CONCERNED 133

the ideas of Wesley could be and were impressed and expressed. Nothing was vague and nothing was left to chance.[42]

It is impossible to understand Methodism or to be able to estimate its significance as a socializing force unless the great importance of its discipline is appreciated. We have seen that it had its roots in Wesley, a man believing in, desiring and seeking, as well as practising, discipline for himself; we have also seen something of the widespread and ever-continued nature of this discipline in the Societies he founded. It will not, therefore, be strange to find the same discipline exercised in respect of the constantly growing body of his preachers. They did not escape, neither collectively nor personally. At the Conference every year, questions of discipline were discussed, the revision of its rules, and the examination into the lives and work of the preachers. Sometimes this latter examination assumed great proportions. At the Conference, for instance, which was held in 1759, almost the whole time of its meeting, some four days, was spent in examining the lives and conduct of the preachers.[43] Often, Wesley had to work hard to maintain the enthusiasm of his preachers without letting it degenerate into enthusiasm in the eighteenth-century meaning of the term. The Maxfield-Bell episode is an illustration. Maxfield, an episcopally ordained preacher, and Bell, a preacher who was a corporal of the King's Life-guards, had become extravagant in their teaching, antinomian in fact, and also extravagant in their actions. Wesley writes a long letter to Maxfield bluntly telling him what

[42] Wesley's correspondence has many letters on the subject of discipline and instruction through Bands and other small groups. Illustrations of such letters will be found in *Letters*, VI.383; VII.47, 139, 247, 291, 324; VIII.57, 99, 261.

[43] *Journal*, IV.348.

it is he disliked, and also some things of which he approved. Two or three weeks later, Wesley, secretly, listens to Bell's conduct of a service, and afterwards severely criticizes him. A week or two later he notes some improvement and so he 'did not yet see cause to hinder (i.e. remove) him'.[44] A fortnight later, however, he hears Bell again, and again a week afterwards. Bell has got worse and so Wesley 'therefore desired that he would come thither no more '.[45] On another occasion, he writes a letter to Christopher Hopper about the appointment of two preachers and says: 'I will not attempt to guide those who will not be guided by me.'[46] That sentence exactly expresses Wesley's attitude, both toward his preachers and to the ordinary member of a Society—they were required carefully to make up their minds if they would put themselves under his care, and if so, then his word was law. Benson, one of the foremost of the preachers, notes in reference to the thirty-fifth Conference (that of 1778) that Wesley 'dealt closely and plainly with the preachers, setting two aside for misdemeanours'.[47]

The duty of the preachers was often irksome as it was always detailed. They had much preaching to do, yet this formed the smaller part of their labours. They were to be pastors, confessors, and inquisitors, both of adults and children, and all this irrespective of their particular gifts or limitations. There was no functional specialization whereby one man might be primarily a preacher and another chiefly a pastor or a teacher. 'The sum is, Go into every house in course, and teach every one therein, young and old, if they belong to us, to be Christians,

[44] ibid., IV.535–40.
[45] ibid., p. 542.
[46] ibid., V.235n.
[47] ibid., VI.206n.

inwardly and outwardly. Make every particular plain to their understanding. Fix it in their memory. Write it on their heart. In order to do this, there must be line upon line, precept upon precept. I remember to have heard my father asking my mother: "How could you have the patience to tell that blockhead the same thing twenty times over?" She answered: "Why, if I had told him but nineteen times, I should have lost all my labour." What patience, indeed, what love, what knowledge is required for this!'

'Over and above: wherever there are ten children in a Society, spend at least an hour with them twice a week. And do this, not in a dull, dry, formal manner, but in earnest, with your might.'

'"But I have no gift for this." Gift or no gift, you are to do it else you are not called to be a Methodist preacher. Do it as you can, till you can do it as you would.'[48] Of course, many preachers did not like this irksome discipline and caught what Wesley described as 'the fashionable disease—desire of independency' but, as in the case recorded at Quinton, near Birmingham, he dealt with them. At first they were 'very warm' but 'at length agreed to act by the Rules laid down in the *Minutes of the Conference*'.[49] At the Conference of 1786, there were some eighty preachers present. A whole day and a half was spent in considering the characters of some of the preachers, 'whether already admitted or not', i.e. whether old or new preachers.[50] Perhaps the most illuminating case of Wesley's extraordinary powers of direction over these men, many of whom were men of

---

[48] Quoted by W. H. Fitchett, op. cit., p. 368, from Myles, *A Chronological History of the People called Methodists*.

[49] *Journal*, VII.60.

[50] ibid., p. 192.

standing in the Methodist world, and some of distinction outside it, is given by his action taken in London in 1787. The old man, over eighty years of age, arrived from one of his tours to find that the next morning when he went at 5.30 to the service, there was no preacher there, so he took the service himself. At that time there were preachers staying just by in 'the house', that is, the headquarters and hostel of the Societies in London. Upon inquiry from them he found they had overslept through being up too late: 'I resolved to put a stop to this; and therefore ordered that (1) every one under my roof should go to bed at nine; that (2) every one might attend the morning preaching. And so they have done ever since.'[51] The four preachers concerned were Dr. Coke, James Creighton, Samuel Bradburn, and John Atlay. These leading men, for such they were amongst the Methodists, were not only made to go to bed, and get up, at the hour Wesley chose, but, through the publication of his *Journal*, knew that even the least important of the members of the Methodist Societies would be made aware of what had happened.

Another objective test of the effectiveness of Wesley's work arises out of his technique as an evangelist. Considering, as he did, that the world was his parish, he not only believed that he had the right to travel and preach anywhere, but that he had a responsibility to exercise in regard to the selection of places into which he went. He was conscious that 'a dispensation of the Gospel was committed unto him', and this led him to formulate the guiding rule that it was his business, and that of his preachers, not merely to do good, but to do as much good as possible. Therefore he sought out evil to attack it, and gradually evolved set rounds for his preaching. In the early stages, he accepted openings for preaching as

[51] ibid., p. 346.

they appeared, and was always willing to respond as far as possible to requests to visit other places. But he had a sense of evangelistic strategy, so that we find him deciding upon three bases, London, Bristol, and Newcastle, for his campaign against the forces of evil. The measure of serious opposition which he gained, especially in the first twenty years of his work after 1738, show how he was carrying this out, for he could have chosen places where he could have worked with acceptance and with little opposition. To him, opposition was a sign of the devil being present and active, and that meant a sign that he had found a place in which the power of the Holy Spirit might be demonstrated. So, Wesley goes repeatedly into areas which were turbulent and often anything but law-abiding. Years after, we find the same places figuring again and again in the *Journal* with remarks, far too numerous to mention, that their character had now changed and the people had become peaceful and law-abiding. As a steadying social force this consideration is not without importance.

It is important to notice that while the Methodist discipline was of great effect in producing a well-regulated and orderly leaven in hundreds of places up and down the country, its severity did not have the effect it might have had of crushing independence and initiative. On the contrary: because the Bands and Classes into which the membership was organized were small, often less than ten in any one. In these small groups the members met every few days and recounted their trials and temptations, and also their victories and joy. In other words, from the social point of view, they became articulate, learning to express themselves, to analyse themselves, and to relate their religious experience to their social duties. It was a form of adult education, not in the nature of a liberal education, it is true, but a real training in citizenship. Further, these Classes being numerically small, there was a corresponding need for more leaders, and anyone who showed an aptitude for leadership had his chance.[52] He might occupy a very low place in the economic scale while being, in a minor way, a religious director to his little circle, and, as we have seen, a religious director in the Methodist Societies was also a social director. By the end of the eighteenth century there were just over 100,000 members of these Societies, which meant, in terms of Band and Class leaders, and also stewards and trustees, something like 10,000 men and women trained to a real, though for the most part limited, leadership.

In spite of local leadership and disciplinary ideals and practice, no doubt many were attracted into these Societies by motives not primarily religious. There is some degree of truth in the contention of a not very sympathetic writer that ' the great attraction of Methodism was that it brought companionship, hope and comfort to the outcast and to the wretched. Those people—with whom none had ever concerned themselves before and who found unexpected delight in gathering together, in attracting the interested attention of preachers and teachers, in discussing with one another their hopes and fears and the state of their souls—found themselves for the first time important, in their own eyes and in those of other people.'[53] Such motives may well have influenced some adherents, but they only emphasize the social appeal and importance of the fellowship and training provided by the Wesleyan Societies.

---

[52] At Bristol, in 1739, the occupations of two out of three Band leaders are given. One was a haberdasher, and the other a barber (see *Letters*, I.296).

[53] Marjorie Bowen, *Wrestling Jacob*, op. cit., pp. 255-6.

Another, and still more unsympathetic, writer was Toplady, but the evidence he brings only confirms the view that these Societies offered a very real and important opportunity for self-expression and leadership to those who would otherwise have lacked such a thing. Toplady says, bitterly: ' the plan (now adopted by Mr. John Wesley ...) was ... that of prostituting the ministerial function to the lowest and most illiterate mechanics, persons of almost any class, but especially common soldiers, who pretended to be pregnant with " a message from the Lord ".'[54] He goes on later: ' Let him (i.e. Wesley) not fight by proxy. Let his cobblers keep to their stalls. Let his tinkers mend their vessels. Let his barbers confine themselves to their blocks and basons. Let his bakers stand to their kneading-troughs. Let his blacksmiths blow more suitable coals than those of controversy.'[55] Toplady also refers to Wesley's ' ragged regiment of lay preachers ',[56] but this is not to be taken literally, for anything in the nature of untidiness Wesley would not in the least permit.

Another contemporary sidelight on the association of Methodist preachers and the socially insignificant comes from Goldsmith's play, *She Stoops to Conquer*. In it, the young Squire, speaking of an inn and its bedroom accommodation, says that there are already in the bed ' two Methodist Preachers and a chimney sweep '. However unfavourable might be the view of some educated persons on the chance for local prominence which Methodism gave to many who would not otherwise have had it, they did not fail to observe the phenomenon.

Nor were these opportunities for self-development and

[54] Augustus Toplady, Works, p. 266.
[55] ibid., p. 279.
[56] ibid., p. 762.

social leadership confined to men. Wesley was easily the most outstanding feminist of the eighteenth century, for he provided opportunities for women nowhere else available for them, except for the very few. Also, these opportunities were based upon his belief in their equality with men before God and that it was in the Divine purpose that they should be used in Methodism. Thanks to the vision and work of George Fox in the previous century, female Friends had achieved a remarkable position, while now amongst the far more numerous Methodists, the women gained a position approximating to that among the Friends. All this arose out of Wesley's experience in the evangelical revival, and he characteristically sums it up in this fashion: ' God owns women in the conversion of sinners, and who am I that I should withstand God ? '[57] From that point the way was open for women to become Band and Class leaders in any Methodist Society, while a number more or less regularly itinerated with Wesley up and down the country, and over to Ireland. Women like Grace Murray, whom he once contemplated marrying, Mary Bosanquet, Ann Cutler, and Hester Rogers, were known over wide areas, the first-named of these actually itinerating with Wesley on and off for ten years.

These opportunities given to ordinary, and often quite obscure, men and women were essentially social. With due regard for the strongly marked individualistic note in the revival led by Wesley, it was to a social fellowship that they were called. They were to be greatly concerned with the salvation of their own souls, but never to the point of excluding, or even forgetting, others. ' No true Methodist ever wanted to go to heaven by himself alone. He did not think of men crossing the river one by one, as Bunyan described them. He sang:

[57] Townsend, Workman and Eayrs, *A New History of Methodism*, I.322.

Part of the *host* have crossed the flood,
  And part are crossing now.

It was a society from the first. . . . No picture is more graphic than Charles Wesley's great fellowship hymn. . . .

All praise to our redeeming Lord,
  Who joins us by His grace,
And bids us, each to each restored,
  Together seek His face.
The gift which He on one bestows,
  We all delight to prove;
The grace through every vessel flows
  In purest streams of love.
Even now we think and speak the same,
  And cordially agree;
Concentred all, through Jesu's name,
  In perfect harmony. . . .

These verses present a perfect picture of a Methodist class meeting of early days.'[58]

Such opportunities for leadership for many, and of fellowship for all, meant the development of responsibility, in a social as well as a religious sense, amongst the poorer classes at a period when there was little else to encourage it. An objective test of this is to some extent provided by the well-known part which Methodists played in the nineteenth century in Trade Union organization and leadership, most notably amongst the Durham miners, but widely elsewhere. This was the maturing, as the stimulus of the Industrial Revolution provided the opportunity, of the long training begun by Wesley.

'The social spirit of the new religious order overflowed into occupational groups. The Methodists were in many

---

[58] J. Ernest Rattenbury, *Wesley's Legacy to the World*, pp. 283-4. These hymns are still sung, and may be found in the most recent *Methodist Hymn Book*, that of 1933, numbered respectively 824 and 745. The latter is still very popular amongst Methodists.

cases the original members of workmen's societies which developed later into Trade Unions. They were accused of meeting in private houses, and forming plans for advancing wages. Out of this activity arose the common charge of sedition, and the names of Brunswick and Hanover were given to many Methodist Chapels as a public proof of loyalty.'[59] These men were far removed from anything in the nature of sedition and proved to be a stabilizing force in the country. ' It is interesting to remark ', says another account, ' the note struck by the committee when appealing to weavers to join the Union (i.e. an Association of Journeymen Weavers of Rochdale, about 1819), " In order that you may become men ".'[60] It may fairly be said that the Methodist Societies had the effect in a great many cases of making men, not only by their religious work and by their emphasis upon ethical standards, but also by the social opportunities they provided. They gave responsibility to men who had generally been regarded as unworthy of any responsibility which involved initiative.[61]

Another indication of the utility, from the social and economic point of view, of the life of the Methodist Societies, comes from the number of those who advanced in economic status. Not only Wesley's *Journal*, but other Methodist literature of the period made reference not

[59] Sydney G. Dimond, *The Psychology of the Methodist Revival*, pp. 222-3, referring to *Home Office Papers*—' Letter from the Vicar of Sandal '. See also J. L. and B. Hammond, *The Town Labourer*, p. 277.

[60] J. L. and B. Hammond, *The Skilled Labourer, 1760-1832*, p. 166.

[61] It may be added also that it gave responsibilities to men who, if they lived in large towns at all events, had only a short expectation of life here. As illustration of this, we may take the gravestones lying round Carver Street Methodist Chapel, Sheffield : recorded on these are the ages of 220 persons ; of them one half failed to reach their twenty-seventh birthday, and one third died before their ninth birthday, the period being early nineteenth century.

infrequently to the growth of Society members in wealth, a growth not always noted with approval. Regarding this, Wesley wrote in 1789: 'The Methodists grow more and more self-indulgent because they grow rich. Although many of them are still deplorably poor . . . yet many others in the space of twenty, thirty, or forty years, are twenty, thirty, yea, a hundred times richer than when they first entered the Society.'[62] These men who were thus disciplined and imbued with Wesley's religious conception of responsibility, with its practice of frugality and hard work, and who had their powers of mind brought out in Band and Class meeting, went ahead in trade and accumulated wealth. It is not without significance that by 1799 it was found necessary to issue a new rule for the Methodist Societies, a rule which said: 'As some of our people have, in different parts of the kingdom, been imposed on, in various ways, by swindlers, who professed themselves members of our Society, let no person be received into any Society, without a certificate, signed by one of the itinerant Preachers.'[63] The Societies which, in earlier days, had been held up to ridicule as associations of those at the bottom of the social and economic scale, are now, soon after the death of Wesley, of sufficient importance to become objects of those who dishonestly sought to obtain charity.

[62] Quoted in J. H. Overton, op. cit., p. 210.
[63] Jonathan Crowther, op. cit., p. 245.

www.ingramcontent.com/pod-product-compliance
Lightning Source LLC
Chambersburg PA
CBHW050827160426
43192CB00010B/1926